How to Draw
ANIME
Characters

Step by Step Guide to
Draw Your Own Original
Characters From Simple
Templates | Includes

MANGA & CHIBI

FLUFFELS HOUSE

"Scan the Code to Download Your
Free Digital Copy of
How to Draw Anime Characters"

You Can Print the Pages and
Give Them Away as Often as
You'd Like!

Table of Contents

"In drawing, nothing is better than the first attempt."
— Pablo Picasso

Introduction

At some point in your life, you may have started to wonder, "Is it really worth my time learning how to draw anime?". Well...of course it is! Anime is a great art style for many reasons, one of which is that it can be very easy to learn and master, even if you've never drawn before in your life. All you need is a little practice and the proper guidance, and that's what this book is all about.

Globally, the term 'anime' has become associated with a specific art style most commonly used in Japanese animations. Like most other art forms, the anime style has a few key elements that separate it from all others but is still very diverse. Anime may seem like a tricky art style to use initially, but even if you're a newcomer who has never drawn anything more complex than a stick figure, it's still possible to master the art of drawing anime with a bit of patience and some practice.

Anime and manga are fantastic mediums through which you can express yourself, craft interesting stories, and grow creatively. There are so many different styles and genres of anime from which to explore and learn. Even if you don't want to create anime specifically, studying different anime styles can also help you find inspiration and develop your own art style to be a little more appealing. The anime style can also be a great learning tool, as creating anime still uses basic drawing techniques, follows the same rudimentary rules as many other art styles, and an average understanding of human anatomy is needed to create more effective character designs.

Even if drawing anime and manga only starts as making fan art or having a fun hobby, it has the potential to become a great passion and can even become a career! Despite its Japanese origins, you don't need to be Japanese to become a successful mangaka and create popular manga and anime. You'd be surprised at some of the extremely popular anime that were created by artists from all over the world, like "Megas XLR", "Voltron: Legendary Defenders", "Teen Titans", and the 'Avatar' series that were created in America, 'W.I.T.C.H.' and 'Radiant' from France, and "Dr. Stone" from South Korea. No matter where you come from, anime can become a gateway to live out your passion and make a living while you're at it!

It doesn't matter if you're a beginner with dreams of one day creating your own manga/anime, a professional artist looking to try out something new and expand their horizons, an anime fan hoping to learn the secrets behind the designs of the characters they love, or someone who has fallen in love with the style and wants to learn how to draw these kinds of characters; this book is has something for everyone! Your age and experience don't matter since it's never too early or too late to start working on a new skill or improving the ones you already have. Even if you don't consider yourself an 'artist', you can still learn to draw anime characters with a little guidance and practice.

Yoshito Publishing is a company that has spent more than 10 combined years helping young, budding artists learn and master a craft they love. All of our experts have studied various types of art for years, and we take great care to make sure our readers find all the information they need. Everyone here at Yoshito Publishing has a burning passion for teaching. We want to help people worldwide find a positive outlet for their creativity and build a possible career in something they truly enjoy. Even those who don't think of themselves as 'artists' still have great potential and only need a helping hand to guide them; we would be honored to be that hand.

In this book, you will learn some of the fundamentals of creating characters using the anime style. This book will help you prepare everything you need, teach you some basic skills applicable to both anime and other art styles, and give you step-by-step guidelines to help you learn and improve your anime art skills. We will start by helping you understand some of the fundamentals, like shading techniques, basic proportions, choosing the best colors, and several beginner exercises to improve your line and artwork in general; all so that even the most inexperienced beginner won't feel lost, confused, or inadequate. We will also be looking at how to create some of the most common anime archetypes to help you better understand how different techniques and elements are used for different character types. This will help you make some incredible anime characters and bring them to life on your page. Lastly, we will share some of the best tips, tricks, and secret techniques to make your art look professional.

Prepare Yourself

Before you start creating your anime designs, it's important to make sure you've prepared your workplace and all the materials you'll need. Creating great anime takes time, patience, organization, and the right mindset. Nothing is more destructive towards the creative process than dropping everything in the middle of your project to rummage through all your supplies to look for a different pen or pencil, only to discover that you don't have everything you need. Having all the drawing materials and devices gathered together and understanding how they work helps you save time, stay motivated, and improve the flow of your whole process.

Pencils

All great drawings and designs begin with a pencil and a piece of paper. They are easy to use and have erasers if you make any mistakes, making them great for planning and doing base work.

There are two different types of pencils, namely regular "wooden pencils" and "mechanical pencils."

Wooden Pencils

These are your regular pencils and are probably the most common writing implement in the world. Wooden pencils are commonly used in the beginning phases of planning and construction work of your drawing. This is mainly because the beginning stages don't require very fine lines or detailed work, and they can be

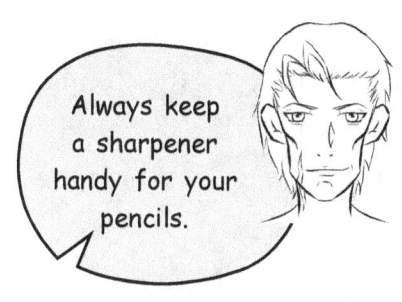

Always keep a sharpener handy for your pencils.

very easy to erase. Wooden pencils are also an essential tool for shading. However, this type of pencil has a "fatal flaw," which is the need to be sharpened. As you work with pencils, they will eventually lose their fine point and need to be sharpened relatively often.

Mechanical Pencils

Mechanical pencils have mostly the same purpose as regular pencils. These are usually used for precise linework and finer details. The main reason for this is that the thickness of the lead remains constant. Having a consistent line can make a world of difference, especially when it comes to

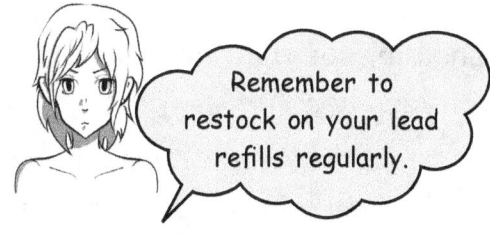

Remember to restock on your lead refills regularly.

small details that become lost if your line is too thick. The biggest problem is that mechanical pencils can't be used to cover large areas effectively. Mechanical pencils also tend to cut into the paper a little if you use too much pressure and can be a little more challenging to erase.

Hard and Soft Lead

The lead inside your pencil, whether wooden or mechanical, can be hard, soft, or somewhere in between.

Hard pencil lead leaves a small amount of graphite behind on the paper when you draw. This means that the line you make with a hard pencil will be very light, and the harder the pencil, the lighter the mark it leaves. This makes the markings very easy to erase. These markings can be used for both the planning and construction phase of your drawing as well as for extremely faint shading.

Soft pencil lead leaves a lot of graphite behind, meaning marks on paper are naturally darker. The softer the pencil, the darker the mark it makes. These dark lines make soft pencils great for linework that needs to be more visible and are great for strong, intense shading. Soft pencils are also easier to blend, and you can get a much wider range of light and dark depending on the pressure you use. The big problem is that soft lead smudges easily and can stick to your hand.

Pencil lead that is somewhere between hard and soft blends the effects of both and is best for your more delicate shading and contouring.

Your pencil or lead refill will be numbered according to the hardness of the lead. Here is the numbering system used globally: 9H down to H, F, HB, and B up to 9B.

'9H' is the number used to indicate the hardest pencil lead currently on the market. '9B' is the softest. As the number of the 'H' pencils goes lower, the pencils become softer, and as the number of the 'B' pencils goes down, the pencils become harder. They will meet in the middle at 'HB' and 'F', which are your medium pencils.

Dip Pen Nibs

Once the planning and pencil sketches are complete, it's time to move to the next stage and ink your artwork. There are many different tools and techniques to do this, but the most popular and versatile way is to use ink and dip pens. There are hundreds of different nibs available on the market, ranging from basic writing and calligraphy nibs to those explicitly created for manga and art.

Choosing the right nibs can be a little intimidating, but there are a few properties to take into consideration:

- **Line-Width:** Depending on how you hold them and how much pressure you apply, a pen nib can produce a large variety of lines with different widths.

- **Flexibility:** This refers to a nib's ability to bend and widen as you apply more pressure, which can improve the quality of your lines a great deal, but too much flexibility in your nib can make your work look messy.

- **Elasticity:** The elasticity of a nib refers to how quickly and easily the nib jumps back to its original shape as you ease the pressure. A nib with high elasticity will go from very thick to very thin quickly and suddenly, while a nib with low elasticity will change slowly and have a more consistent line-width in general.

Knowing the width, flexibility, and elasticity of a pen nib just by looking at it in the packaging is impossible, so here are some of the nibs most commonly used for creating manga and anime to help you get started:

G Nib

This is the superstar of manga-drawing nibs and is used by most artists. It has a fair amount of flexibility and elasticity. You can find both harder and softer G nibs, making it great for both professionals and beginners.

School Nib

This nib is perfect for beginners. It's a reasonably hard nib that creates consistent lines, but it does have some flexibility and elasticity, making it an excellent tool to practice creating variation in your lines. It's also a small, short nib, which further helps in making it easy to control.

Spoon Nib

This is another nib for beginners and can be identified by its iconic shape that gives it its name. This nib has almost no flexibility, resulting in very consistent lines. It usually makes thin lines, but it can be tilted on its side to make thicker ones. Most artists prefer to use this nib for scenery and inanimate objects.

Mapping Nib

This nib creates extremely thin lines, making it great for finer details. The lines stay relatively thin and consistent, even if you apply a lot of pressure. One problem with this nib is that it is small and isn't compatible with many nib holders.

Soft Mapping Nib

This nib combines the delicate, thin lines of the mapping nib with the flexibility and expressiveness of the G nib. This pen works best for drawing details that use long, curving lines, such as long hair and soft fabric. It's best to get a little practice in before using this nib.

Japanese Nib

This is the jack-of-all-trades among the manga nibs. It's more flexible and elastic than a school or spoon nib but less than a G nib. It has great flow and maneuverability but still creates consistent lines and isn't too difficult to control. This makes it great for most types of drawing and is a good option if you don't want to use a lot of different nibs.

Nib Holder

While the nib holder is simply a tool to cradle your nib and make working with it practical, you should still take some time to choose the right one. No matter which material you prefer, you should be sure you use a comfortable holder that feels right in your hand. Also, make sure your holder is compatible with your nibs!

Ink

Once you have your nibs together, you should find the ink suitable with which to work. Different types of ink react in different ways to your nibs and paper, and you should take some time to find the ink you like to work with the best.

When buying ink, you will need to look at how thick or thin the ink is and how easily it flows from your pen. It's always best to get high-quality ink, as your inkwork will have the most significant influence on your final artwork. An excellent way to test the quality of your ink is to make a brushstroke on a piece of paper with a fine paintbrush. If your ink produces a solid, opaque line with a good, black color, the ink is of great quality and can be used for your art.

India Ink

India ink was created initially in China and has been used for thousands of years. It is still one of the most commonly used ink types and comes in many different forms. India ink is made primarily from carbon and is usually waterproof. Typically, India ink is slightly shiny.

Drawing Ink

Drawing ink refers to any type of ink oriented for drawing and creating artwork rather than just writing. Drawing ink can be divided into two primary groups, namely dye-based ink and pigment-based ink.

"Dye-based ink" uses materials that dissolve in water and dye the paper. Dye inks tend to take some time to dry and are absorbed into the paper. They work well with brushes, dip pens, and airbrushes. Dye inks are usually waterproof, but they tend to fade after prolonged exposure to light. India ink is a prime example of dye-based ink.

"Pigment-based inks" use a carrier that places color pigment onto the paper. They are a little thicker than dye inks and tend to act a lot like acrylic paint. Pigment inks tend to work best with paintbrushes, and you will have to thin them out a little if you want to use them with dipping pens or an airbrush. These types of ink are usually very opaque and vibrant, are less likely to fade from exposure to light, and dry quickly, but they are generally just water-resistant. The most common example of a pigment ink is acrylic ink.

Industrial Ink

This type of ink is used for printing projects like linoleum printing and can be a great way to recreate the same image more than once. There are many different types of industrial inks that are used for a variety of techniques. Industrial ink is also the best option to use if you want to work on more unconventional surfaces, like plastic.

Special Inks

These inks can fall into any of the categories mentioned above, but they are specially created to enhance or alter their properties for a specific purpose. Some good examples are inks like "IC Comic Super Black" or "Kuretake Manga Black," which are explicitly designed for manga and comics. These inks tend to be a lot darker, become matte and smudge-proof when they dry, and do not bleed as quickly as many of your cheaper inks.

Other Inking Tools

There are many other ways to ink your work besides dip pens, and it's up to you to decide with what tool you would like to work. Once again, you should try to invest in higher-quality inking tools for a better result, and I will share some of my favorite brands to help you get started.

Paintbrush

This is the most traditional inking tool and has a lot of flexibility and elasticity. A paintbrush can create a wide variety of lines and can even be used for shading. However, it is very tricky to control, and you need a good deal of practice before mastering this tool. High-quality brushes use natural hair rather than synthetic, and the best use sable hair.

Fineliners

These pens, often also referred to as 'rapidographs', are another very popular inking tool. They have a plastic or fiber tip that delivers ink to your paper in an excellent, even line. They are elegant and clean to use, and the ink dries instantly. Fineliners have no flexibility, but they are effortless to maneuver, making them great for beginners. They also come in a wide variety of line-width. The best brands for fineliners are 'Sakura', 'BXT', 'Koh-I-Noor', and "Boa Core".

Brush Pens

A brush pen combines the clean, easy lines of a fineliner with the flexibility and elasticity of a paintbrush. A brush pen can create very dynamic, expressive lines, but it can be a little challenging to control. The best brands for brush pens are 'Tombow', 'Pentel', and "Docraft Artiste".

Illustration Markers

Markers are another tool that uses plastic or fiber tips. These tips are usually fairly broad, and illustration markers are mainly used for thick, bold lines to cover large areas and add color. Some brands of colored markers have their ink explicitly designed to let you blend colors for an even better effect. The best brands for both black and colored markers are 'Copic', 'Prismacolor', 'Sakura', and 'Tombow'.

White

Having a tool to add white to your artwork is just as important as black ink. The two main reasons why you need to have white are to correct mistakes you may make with your black ink and to add highlights. There are three ways to add white to your artwork:

Correction Fluid

This is one of the easiest ways to add a solid white to your work and is the best for fixing mistakes. It's simple to use and can be bought in the form of a pen, tape, or a liquid to be applied with a brush. It's very convenient and dries very quickly, but you need to be very careful since it won't have the same texture as the paper. If you reapply ink over correctional fluid, it will look slightly different than the ink applied directly onto the paper.

Paint

Paint is another good way to add white. It's relatively easy to apply, but it takes a while to dry. You should also make sure to have a very opaque type of paint, like gouache or good quality acrylic, and it may be necessary to add a few layers for a solid white color. Thin white paint can also be used to lighten colors slightly.

White Ink

This is specialized pigment ink. White ink can look amazing and can even be layered and blended onto other inks to create soft highlights. White ink tends to be slightly translucent, and you will have difficulty making solid white over black ink.

Paper

Choosing the right paper for your artwork is essential. While standard printing paper can be an excellent paper to practice on, it won't do the job if you want to create professional-looking manga.

First, you should look at the density of your paper. The denser your paper, the heavier it is and the more punishment it can take. This is especially so if you're planning on using ink and nibs or paintbrushes. The density of your paper is indicated on the packaging by a number (e.g., 120 g/m). This signifies the weight of your paper per square meter. The higher the number, the denser your paper.

You should also look at the texture of your paper. It can have either a rough or smooth texture, which will affect the overall look of your work. It may be a good idea to look into illustration boards, as different types of boards are created according to the specific needs of other mediums and art techniques.

Lastly, you should consider the size of your paper. If you're creating manga, you should use 'A4' for a single page and 'A3' for a double page, but if you're simply creating anime artwork, you can use any size that looks good and with which you like working.

Cover the Basics

Before you can start creating your awesome artwork, you need to understand the basics. There are some rudimentary skills and techniques you need in order to improve the quality of your artwork in general, and there is some basic information specific to anime that differs from most other art styles. Mastering the basics will save you a lot of time when it comes to creating your *actual* artwork, as you'll spend a lot less time struggling with the planning and basework phases.

Drawing Exercises

Straight Lines

Straight lines are necessary for any art style, especially with manga and anime. Drawing straight lines without a ruler can be extremely tricky, and the only way to improve is through practice. Here are a few simple techniques that can help you improve your ability to control your lines, and you don't need anything more than a piece of paper and a pencil.

1. **Parallel Lines**: At the top of your page, draw a horizontal line as straight as possible, and try to keep the pressure constant. Draw a line directly underneath with the same force, and try to keep it as straight and as parallel with the previous line as you can. Keep making more lines until you've filled about half a page.

2. **Gradient Parallel Lines:** This is a simple variation of the previous exercise. Start your first line using as much pressure as possible. Draw the following line with slightly less pressure. Make each line slightly lighter than the last, and try to see how gradual you can make the change from dark to light.

3. **Value-Shifting Parallel Lines:** Draw a straight line at the top of your page. Start the line using a lot of pressure and gradually decrease the pressure to change from dark to light. Draw a few lines like this underneath each other, trying to stay parallel. Next, draw a few lines starting with a light line and gradually increase your pressure.

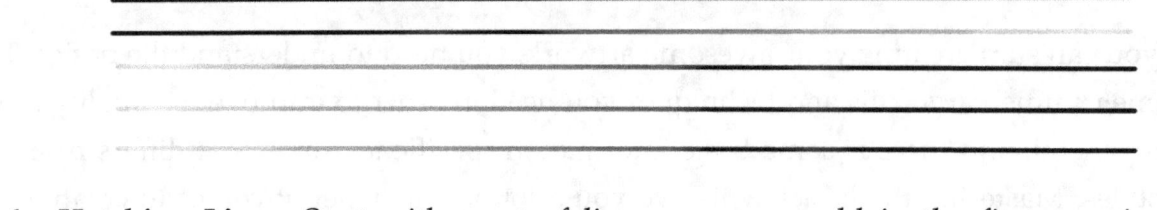

4. **Hatching Lines:** Start with a set of lines as you would in the first exercise. Directly underneath, draw another set in a different direction. As you draw, make sure that you stop along an imaginary edge and keep the space between the end of your line and the last line the same. Keep making sets of lines in different directions to finish the exercise.

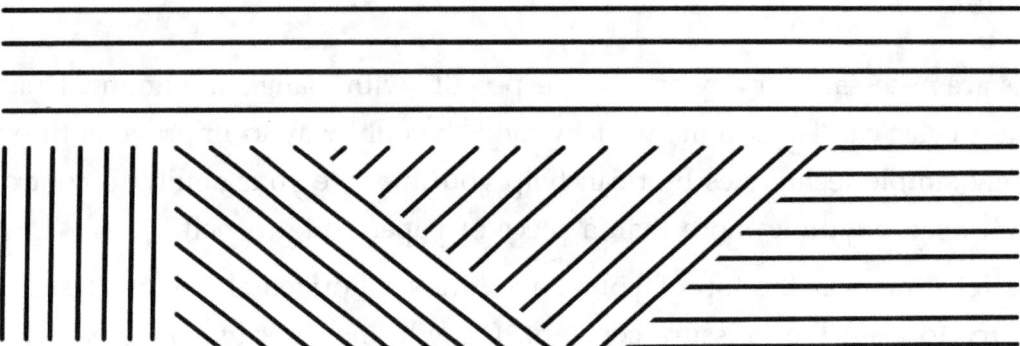

Curved lines

Curved lines are just as important as straight lines and can be deceptively tricky to truly master, but a few exercises can help you improve.

1. **Spiral:** This is a fundamental exercise with which to start. In the center of your page, draw a line that loops around itself to create a spiral; try to draw with steady pressure and keep the curves as smooth and as parallel as possible.

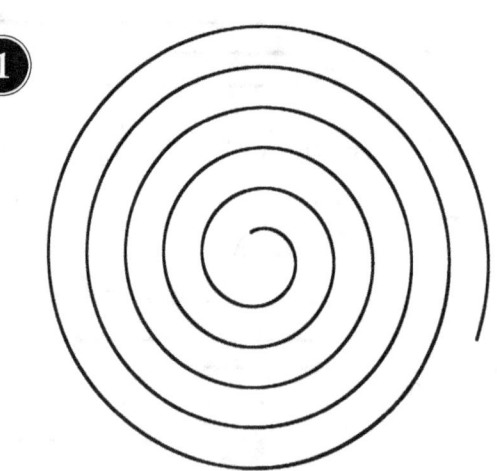

2. **Fixed-Point Spiral:** Choose a side or corner of your page as a starting point, and begin creating a spiral again. This time, as you reach the side where you started, let the line overlap through the starting point rather than keeping the line parallel.

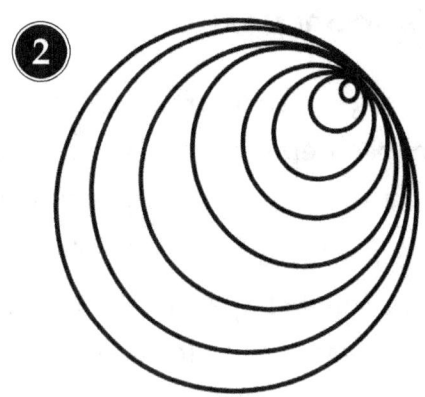

3. **Broken Circles:** For this exercise, start by drawing a small circle in the center of your page. Draw small arcs around the center circle so that they eventually form a series of broken circles outward. If you find this a little too tricky, you can practice drawing regular circles around the center circle first.

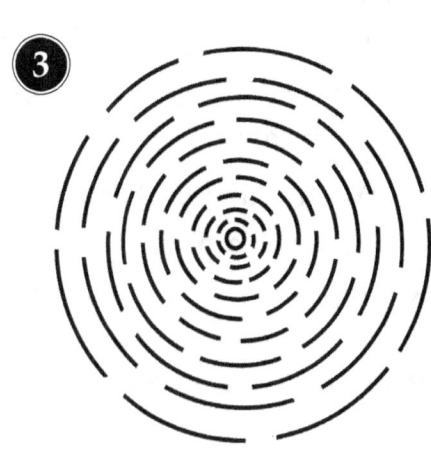

4. **Gradient Circles:** Start by making a small circle on your page using a lot of pressure. Make a slightly larger circle around it using a little less pressure. Keep making slightly larger circles, drawing them lighter and lighter as you go. Once your circles are as light as possible, you can start making them darker again as you fill your page.

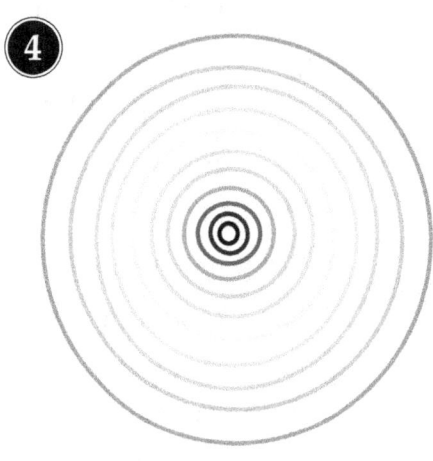

5. **Gradient Spiral:** Just like the first exercise, draw a spiral on your page, but this time, start with a lot of pressure and gradually decrease your pressure to create a smooth gradient.

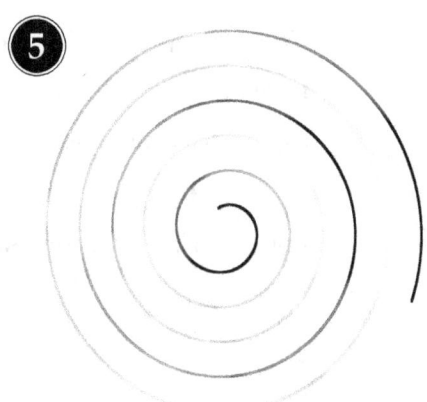

Basic Shapes

A large part of art is combining lines and shapes to create something new. Creating accurate shapes depends largely on pencil control, and you will need to practice a little. An excellent way to practice your pencil control is to draw any shape you like, be it geometric or organic, and trace your pencil over the shape a few times. Try to keep your lines as accurate as possible.

Some shapes, especially circles and ellipses, are exceedingly difficult to get right, and the only way to master them is through repetition. Find and print images of shapes in different sizes and angles, and trace over them a few times. With circles, you should try to trace them clockwise a few times and then change direction. You don't need to rush through these shape exercises. Try to relax, take it slow, and focus on controlling your pencil. You will become faster naturally.

When drawing shapes and lines, you have to remember to use your entire arm. Keep your arm locked and draw by moving your wrist for smaller details, but for larger areas, you should lock your wrist and move your arm by rotating your shoulder.

Advanced Exercises

Once you've practiced your lines, curves, and shapes for a few days, you can move on to something more advanced. These exercises are a great way to grow, and many artists use them to get out of a slump and relieve some pressure.

1. **Different Angles:** Choose an object and make a quick, simple sketch of it. Change the angle you view it from and make another sketch. Make a few of these sketches from different viewpoints.

2. **Blind Drawing:** Choose an object or a scene you want to draw, put your pencil on the paper, and start drawing without looking at your sketch once. Keep your eyes focused on the scene or object you're drawing and not on your hands.

3. **One-liner:** Choose something to draw, either from a reference or from memory, and simply sketch it without lifting your pencil once. Create the whole drawing using one single line. You will have to redraw over lines and plan ahead a little.

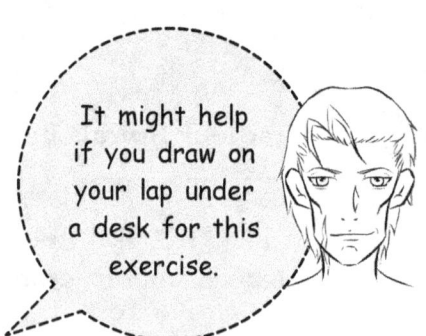

It might help if you draw on your lap under a desk for this exercise.

4. **Different Styles:** Try drawing the same character or scene using different styles.

Heads and Faces

Many of the key elements that set anime apart from other art styles can be found in the face, head, and hair. Because of this, it's very important to understand the basic proportions of the head and face and how to manipulate these into different angles and expressions.

Basic Facial Construction and Proportions

Drawing anime faces is fairly simple, and while the basic construction is very similar to most other styles, there are a few differences to take into account. There are a handful of steps to follow in order to draw a basic face from a frontal view. It's better to start off drawing lightly, as you will have to erase some of the lines later. Using different colored pencils can also help you see what's happening in the different phases.

1. Start with a regular circle. Draw a long, vertical line through the middle of the circle to indicate the center of the face.

2. Divide the circle roughly into thirds horizontally, and draw a line along with the last third on the bottom. This will indicate the middle of the face and can be called the 'eye-line'.

3. Make a small, horizontal line below the center one the same distance as the top half of the head to indicate where the chin will be. This is the 'chin-line'.

4. Draw another horizontal line dividing the lower half of the face in half again so that you have two quarters. This is the 'nose-line'. Divide the lower quarter of the face into half again to create the 'mouth-line'. All the lines you've drawn up to now are called "construction lines".

5. Create the basic shape and placing of the head and face. Where the eye-line meets the edge of the circle, start to draw the side of the face towards the mouth-line. Once you reach the mouth-line, curve inwards and let the line end where your vertical line meets the chin-line. You can make the jaw and chin harder or softer depending on how sharply you turn. You can use sharper lines for the jaw and chin to create a more masculine look and make the jaw wider.

6. To place the eyes, the top of the eye should touch the eye-line. Draw a circle the size of an eye in the center of the face, and draw the eyes on each side.

7. Next, place the nose and mouth. Draw the line of the mouth slightly above the mouth-line. Place the nose so that the tip of it should be directly over the nose-line. Draw in the ears between the eye and nose-lines.

8. Finally, add the final touches such as eyebrows, mouth, and nose details and other distinguishing features.

Draw a small line where the bottom of the eye should be to make it a little easier.

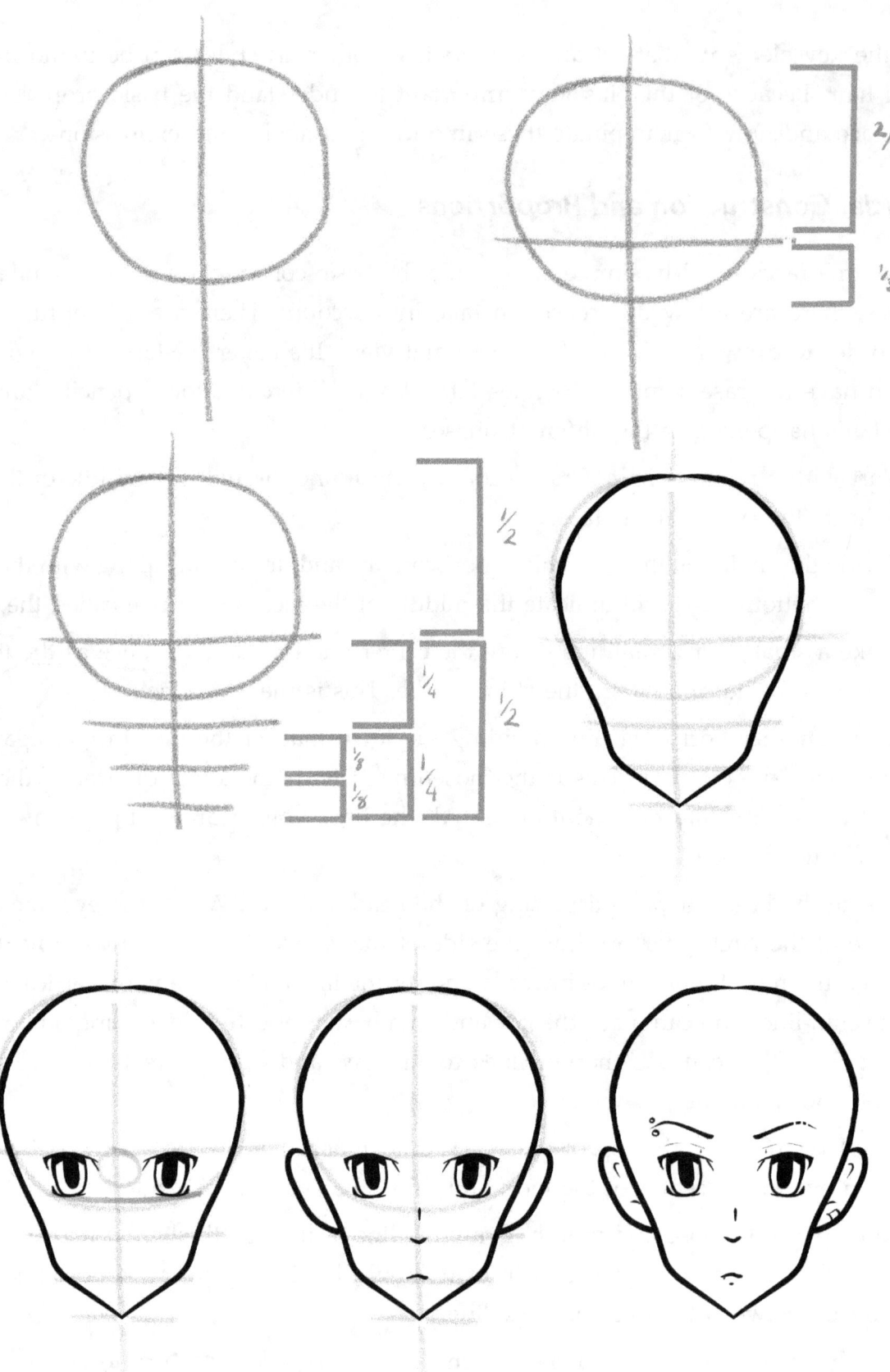

Mapping the Face at Angles

Even if you know the basic proportions of a face, it can still be a little difficult to draw it at different angles. This will take some practice. To help you get a feel for how it works, here's a step-by-step walkthrough on how to do this:

1. Once again, start with a circle. This time, draw the vertical line towards the side of the circle in the direction your character is looking. The line needs to curve with the face, and you should start the line coming from the top-middle of the circle.

2. Divide your circle into thirds again to create the eye-line. The horizontal lines also curve along with the circle in the direction the character is looking.

3. Draw a smaller circle along the edge opposite your center line. Divide the smaller circle in half vertically and horizontally, using the eye-line as a guide.

4. Add the chin, nose, and mouth-lines using the same proportions as you would for a frontal view.

5. Start creating the shape of the face. On the left side, start above the eye-line where the brow would be. As you draw, gently dip the line in under the brow, out of the cheek, and slightly out again near the chin. For the other side of the face, start at the bottom of the smaller circle and curve towards the chin at the mouth-line.

6. Place the eyes and nose without adding too much detail. The eye on the left of the image should be very close to the edge of the face. The tip of the nose protrudes from the center line. The bridge of the nose goes over the eye further back and connects to the brow.

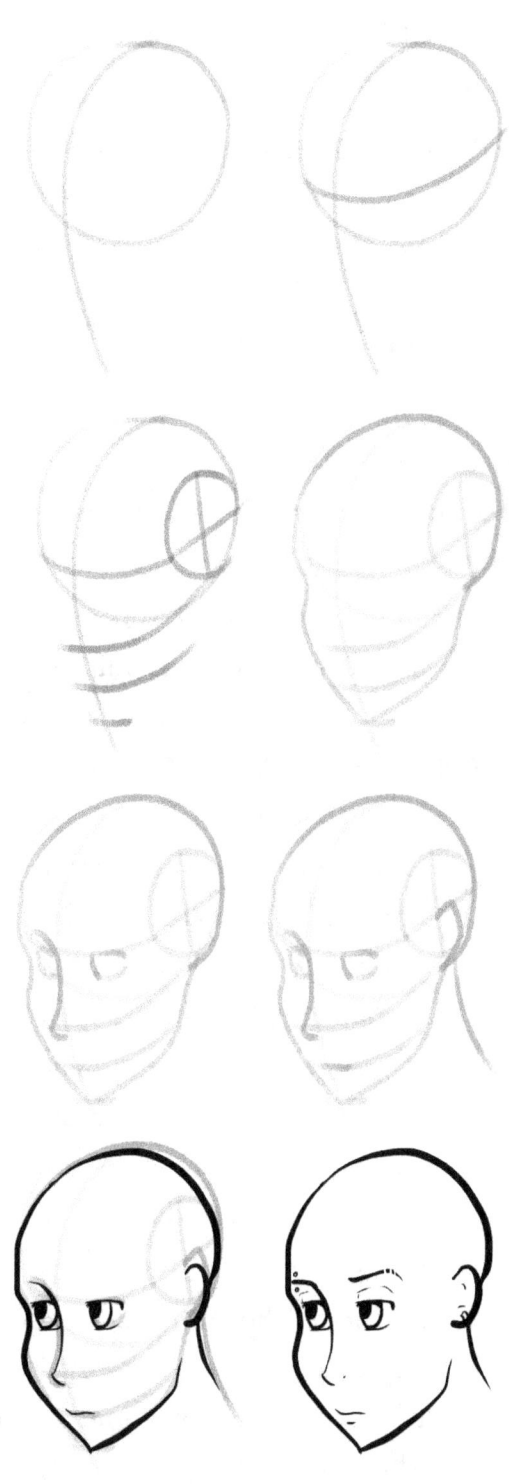

7. Place the mouth on the mouth-line slightly off-center. Use the center point you've marked in the smaller circle and the edge where the circle meets the jaw to place the ear.

8. Strengthen your lines, and give the features a little more definition.

9. Add the final refinement and details.

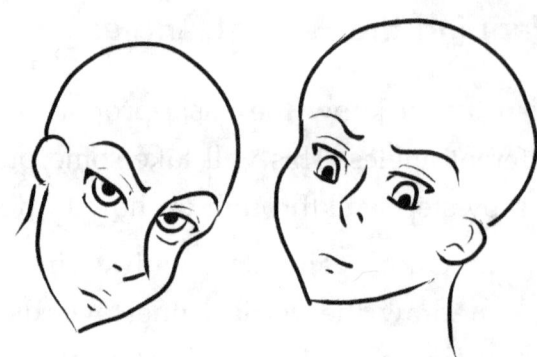

When drawing your faces, don't let the construction lines limit you too much. If something doesn't look right, feel free to change things to suit your style better.

Facial Expressions

Facial expressions are a critical part of creating art that tells a story. Not only do expressions convey the emotions that your character is feeling, but they can also help reveal a little more about their personality. An example is a very positive person who is always smiling and bubbly, or someone with a violent, antisocial personality who always scowls and looks angry.

When drawing anime, three main features of the face are used to portray emotion: the eyes, eyebrows, and mouth. By manipulating these three features, you can let any character portray any emotion. The more intensely you manipulate these features, the more charged the emotions will appear. Here are some of the most common expressions you should master:

1. **Joy:** When expressing joy, the mouth is usually wide, with the corners curving upwards in an open smile or a grin. The bottom of the eye is pushed up a little by the smile, or the eye is completely closed. The eyebrows are relaxed.

2. **Anger:** For anger, the eyebrows arch down towards the center. They are drawn very sharply, and the eyes are squinted. The mouth is drawn fairly wide, with the corners slightly curving downward.

3. **Sadness:** The entire face droops down when expressing sadness. The eyebrows start a little higher in the center and curve downwards. The mouth also has a strong downward slant, and the irises of the eyes will be looking down as well. Adding tears can further help you convey this emotion.

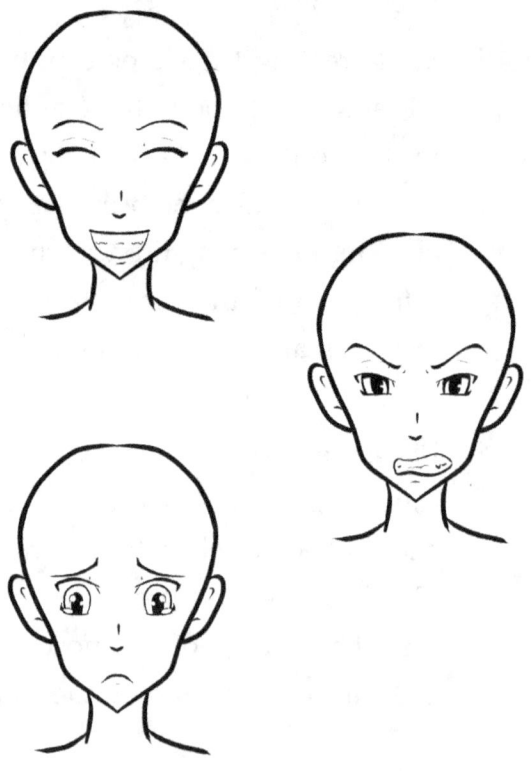

4. **Surprise:** When surprised, the entire face opens and becomes round. The eyebrows are wide, upward arches, and the eyes are opened a little wider. The mouth has an 'O' shape.

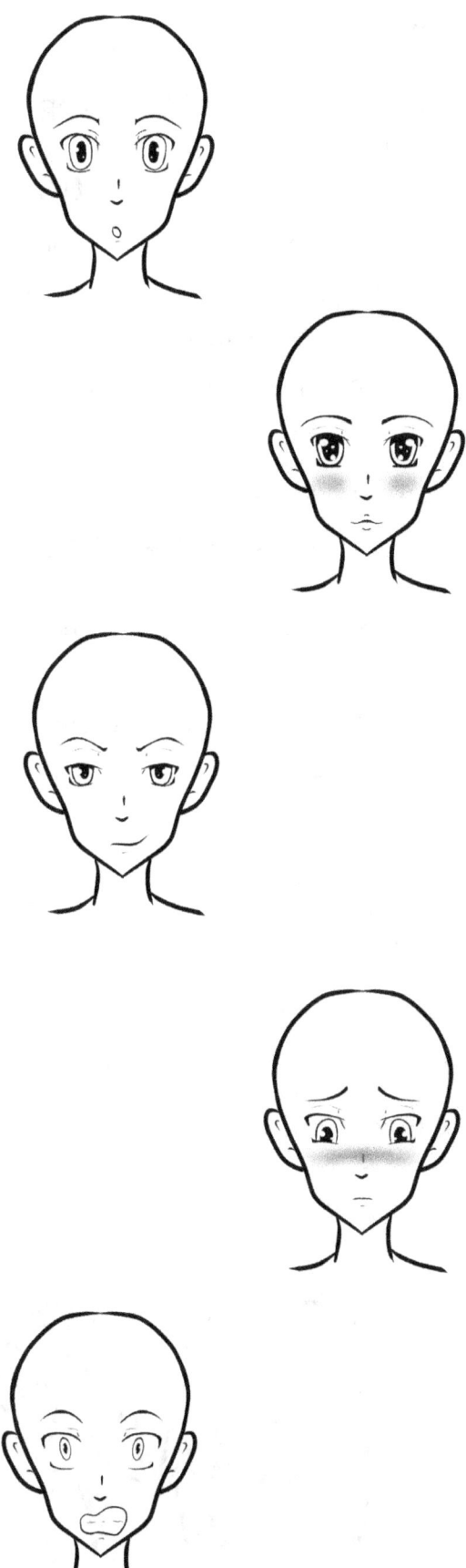

5. **Love:** This is a subtle emotion. The pupils of the eyes are a little larger than normal, and the amount of reflections increases. The eyebrows are relaxed, and the mouth is in a soft, gentle smile. Sometimes, a slight blush is added to the cheeks and nose.

6. **Arrogance:** For this emotion, the eyes are a little closed, and the eyebrows arch down towards the middle. The upper lid of the eye is a little more closed. The mouth is usually a lopsided smile with one corner pulling higher than the other.

7. **Shyness:** The iris of the eye will often be a little to the side or lower. The lower eyelid is a little closed. The eyebrows start a little high and curve downward. The mouth is in a soft smile, a straight line, or slightly pulling down at the corners. Sometimes, blush is applied to the cheeks or entire face.

8. **Fear:** The eyes are open a little wider than normal, and the irises are smaller. The eyebrows are raised. The mouth is usually open in a wide, rounded shape.

It can be helpful to give a little extra attention to the eyes as they can be the most difficult.

Hair

Hair is one of the quickest, simplest ways to give your character a unique, easily identifiable character trait. Hair can either be basic or very complex, and there are hundreds of different styles and hair types from which to choose. Luckily, all these types follow the same steps to draw.

1. It's better to have the construction lines for the face in place for this.

2. Find the crown of the hair, and draw a few strands to help give it direction. This is usually somewhere close to the top center of the head or where the bangs are most prominent on the head.

3. Start drawing your hair by creating a few thicker strands to build shape.

4. Keep adding hair to different areas of the head, working in layers and using large strands.

5. Something important to keep in mind when drawing hair is the direction in which the hair is flowing. This is especially important when drawing hair that is tied back or very curly.

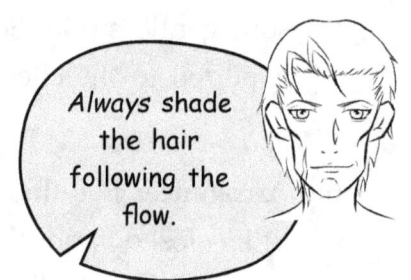

Always shade the hair following the flow.

6. Refine and touch up the strands you've made, and add details.

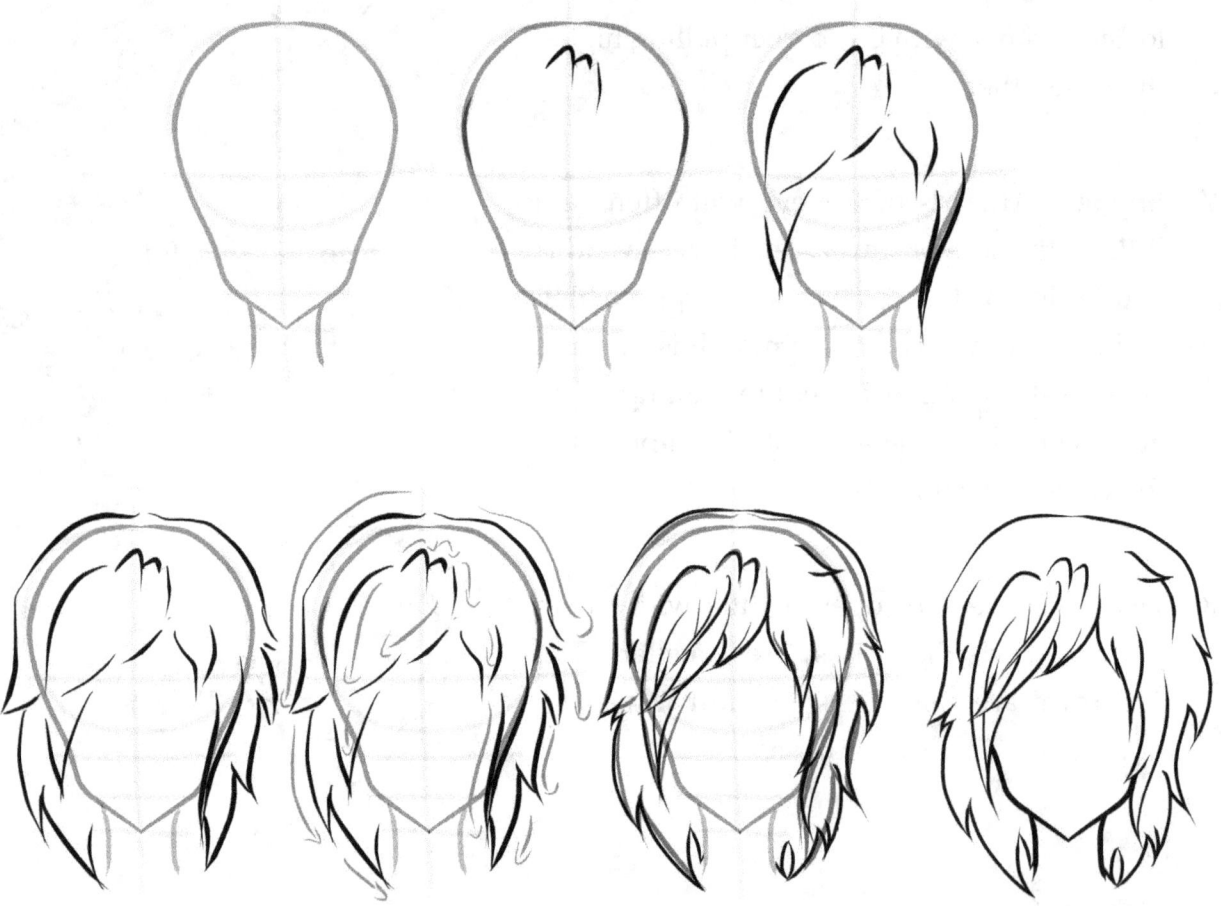

Individual Parts

While you might be excited to start drawing your characters, you might want to practice sketching a few body parts individually to get a little practice first.

Neck and Shoulders

The neck and shoulders can be drawn either simply or with a fair amount of definition and detail.

1. Start at a point somewhere between the jaw and the edge of the chin. Remember that anime necks are thinner than normal. Draw the line of the neck down, making it a little bit wider at the end. Draw a circle to place the shoulder.

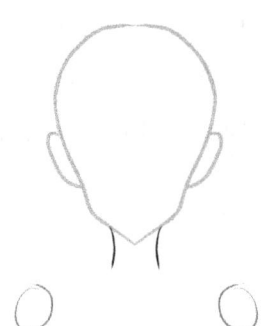

2. Start a little higher than the end of the neck, and draw a line that curves into the trapezius muscle.

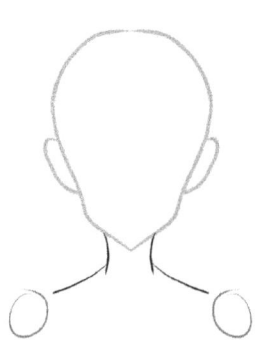

3. Draw a fairly big curve and a line downward to create the shoulder flowing into the arm.

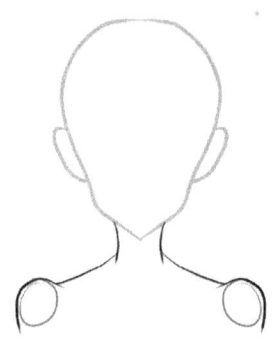

4. Add details such as the collarbones and Adam's apple. The collarbones are relatively high and start close to the center of the chest. Draw them with a diagonal line towards the point where the trapezius muscle and shoulder meet.

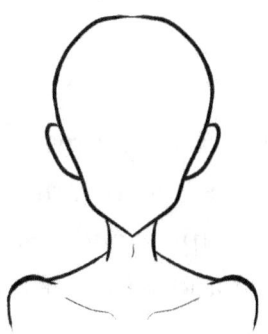

Arms

The arm may seem quite simple to draw, but the difference between an arm that looks just okay and one that looks perfect can make a big enough difference to bring your art to a whole new level.

1. To draw an arm, start by drawing three circles to place the shoulder, elbow, and wrist joints. The distance between the shoulder and elbow as well as elbow and wrist should be the same.

2. Use a few simple lines to connect the joints and form the arm. Make sure your lines aren't too straight and shapeless.

3. Strengthen the outlines of your arm, and add a few more details.

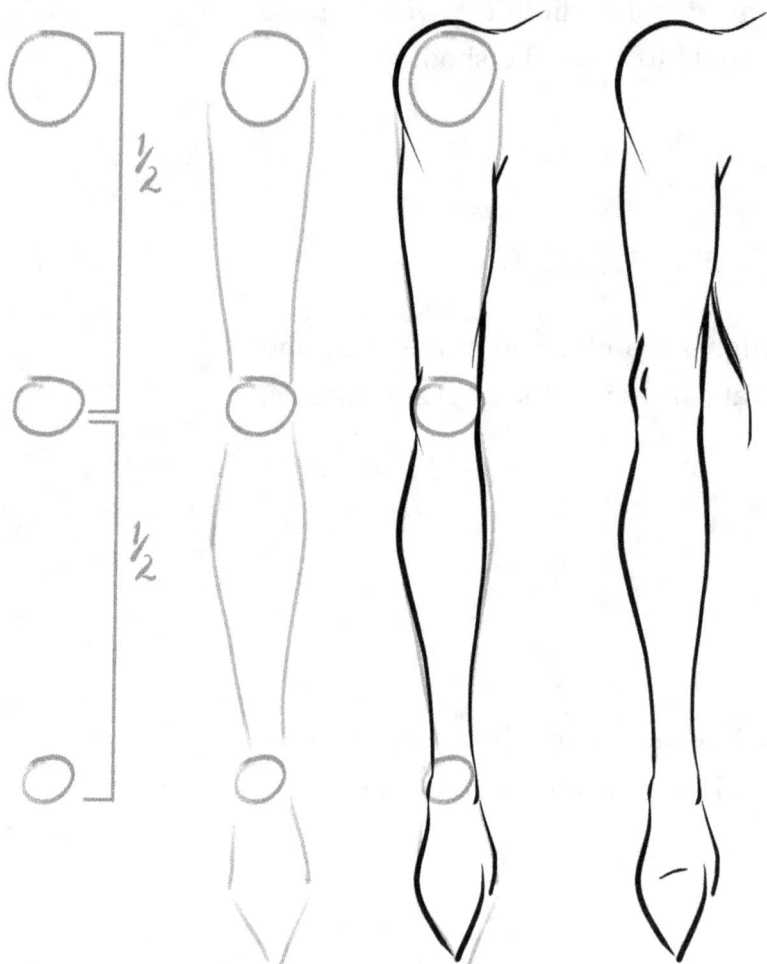

When drawing arms in different poses, there are two important elements to consider: the bend and twist of the arm. As the arm bends, the elbow becomes more prominent, and a fold between the upper and lower arm opposite the elbow becomes more visible. As the arm twists, the position and width of the wrist and elbow change. It's a good idea to use your own arm as a reference.

Hands

Drawing hands is something with which most artists struggle, and it can be challenging to draw a hand that has realistic proportions. Unfortunately, hands are unavoidable, and you can't take the easy way out of hiding your character's hands behind their body or conveniently placed scenery.

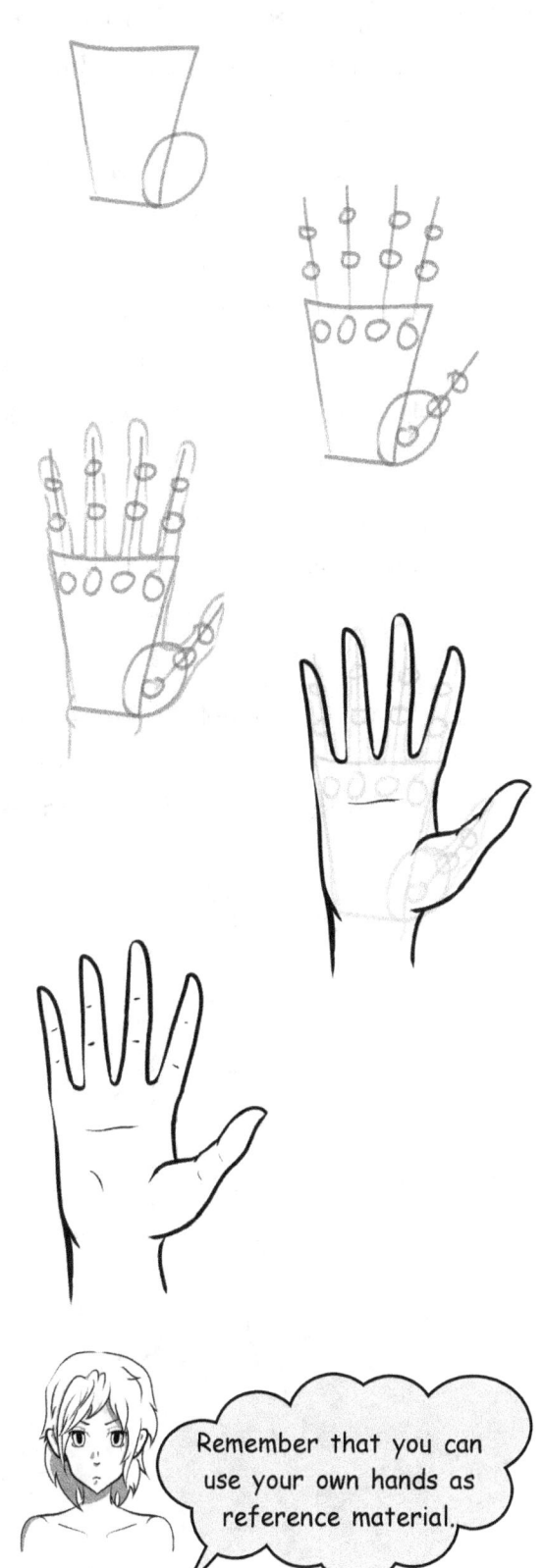

1. Use a rough rectangle and ellipse to draw the base of the hand and the thumb pad.

2. Draw five lines to indicate the fingers' position and then use circles to place the knuckles and joints of each finger. The tip and middle section of the fingers should each be a little shorter than the bottom section.

3. Draw in the basic shape of the fingers. Remember to leave a little space between each finger.

4. Draw the final outline, and add details like fold lines, nails, etc.

Hands can be complicated to draw when they're holding something, but the process is very similar. In Step 1, use a third rectangle-like shape to map out the general area where the fingers will be. Then, draw in the basic shape of the object the hand is holding. There will be a few overlapping lines, but you can erase these later. Follow the rest of the steps, work around the object, and add details to the object in the last step.

The same method is used for drawing male and female hands. The only differences are that female fingers tend to be more slender, while male hands are a little larger in general.

Remember that you can use your own hands as reference material.

Mastering Poses

Anime is a hub of poses that are dynamic and interesting. If you want to be a great artist who tells stories with their work, you will have to learn to draw your characters in as many different poses as possible. The best approach to take when drawing—and especially practicing—poses is the "mannequin technique". In this technique, you map out the entire body before moving on to the finer details like hair, clothing, and faces.

1. Start by drawing single lines to create the base of the pose, and use circles to indicate the joints of the shoulders, elbows, hips, and knees. Use basic shapes to show the position of the head, hands, and feet.

2. Use wedge-like shapes to draw the torso and hips.

3. Add the basic shape of the arms and legs, and connect the torso to the hips and head. If the pose doesn't look right, move the different pieces of the body around until you're happy with the pose.

4. Draw a more definite outline, adding further shape and definition. It's best to start working from the torso outward. You can stop here if you are practicing drawing different poses or adding more details and refining the drawing.

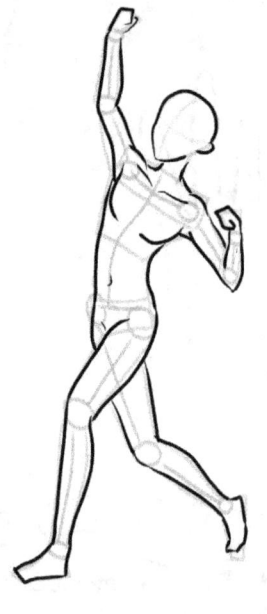

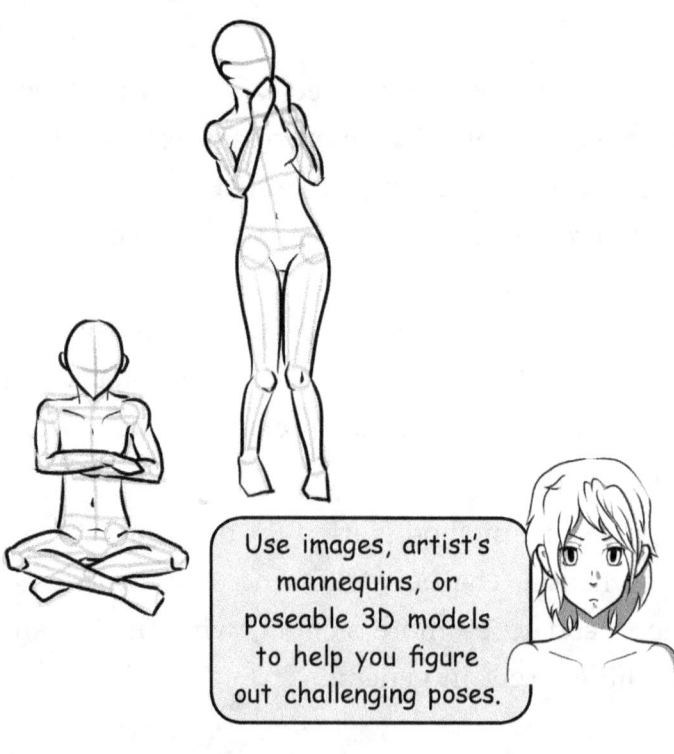

Use images, artist's mannequins, or poseable 3D models to help you figure out challenging poses.

Perspective

Perspective is a very important technique used to give your art depth and dimension and is a critical skill every artist needs and uses frequently. It's even possible that you've drawn something in perspective without realizing it. "Perspective drawing" uses a "vanishing point" to help the artist accurately create depth in their work. Choose a spot on your page to create the vanishing point where the 'distance' renders everything too small to see. Draw lines from the object you are making, like a building, towards the vanishing point. You can then use these lines to accurately draw the sides of the building to look three-dimensional or to judge the size of a similar object further away.

In art, there are four types of perspective drawing: Single-point perspective, two-point perspective, three-point perspective, and foreshortening.

"Single-point perspective" is when the artwork only has one vanishing point. This is mostly used to draw scenery.

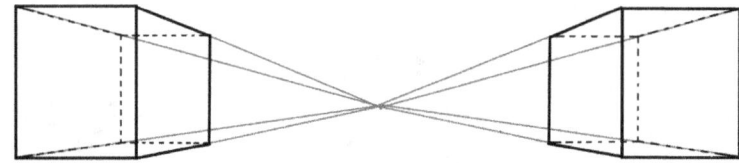

"Two-point perspective" uses two vanishing points, usually on opposite sides of the page, and is generally used for drawing buildings when viewed from a corner.

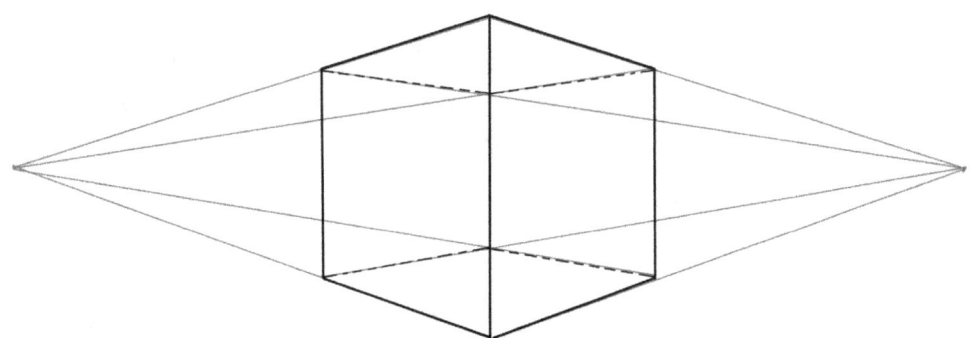

"Three-point perspective" uses three vanishing points. This type of perspective is used very rarely.

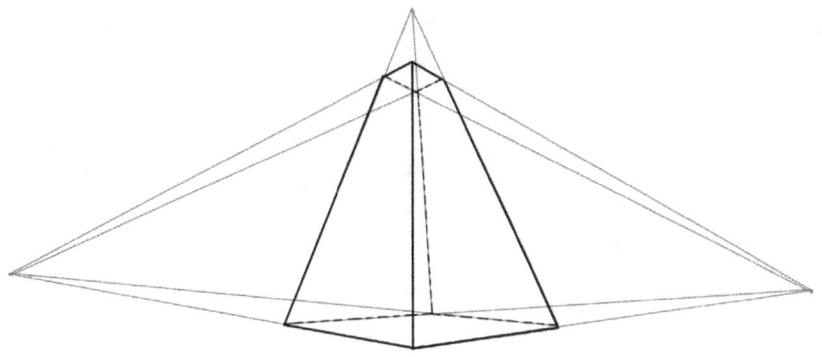

'Foreshortening' is when one part of the body looks larger or smaller than it should be or has a warped shape because it is closer to or further away from you than it should be. You will likely use this the most for your characters, and the best way to improve this technique is by practicing poses that cause foreshortening.

How to Apply Perspective Practically

Other than foreshortening, you will likely use single-point perspective the most. As in the example, you can use this to make objects look three-dimensional or create a room, but it also uses drawing scenes with more than one character. Draw a character somewhere on the page. Then, draw perspective lines from the top and bottom of the character. Choose how far back you want the next character to be, and draw a vertical line between the two perspective lines at that point. This line will show how tall your character should be at this distance.

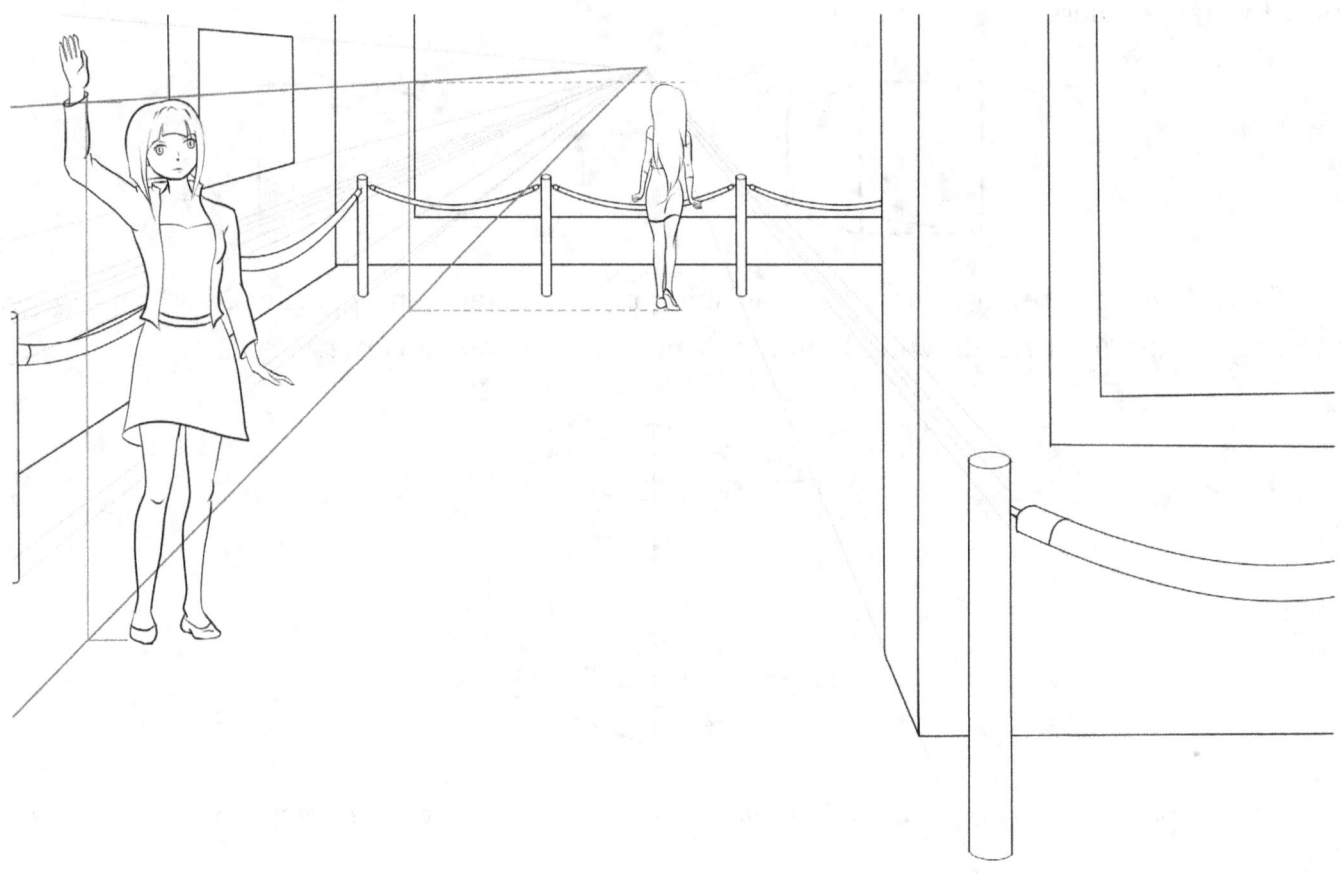

Shading

Shading is another crucial aspect of art if you want to bring your characters to life, and the proper shading can help tell the story of your character. There are many different shading techniques, but we'll be taking a look at the ones most commonly used for manga and anime.

Hatching and Cross-Hatching

Hatching is a technique where you draw small lines next to each other to create a shaded area. The closer the lines are to each other, the darker the shadow will be. This is the most commonly used technique for manga. Cross-hatching works the same way but uses a second layer of lines in the opposite direction to create a gridded shadow area.

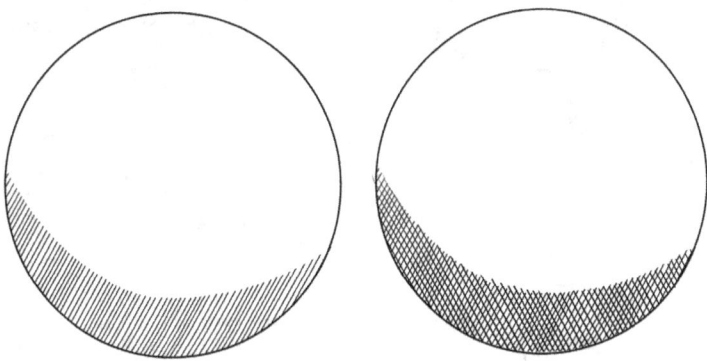

Solid Shading

This is a technique usually used in anime and works by simply applying a darker layer of color to add shading. In most cases, anime will use a solid color with a hard line, but you can use shading with a softer edge that blends with the lighter color underneath for a slightly more realistic look.

Extremely dark shading can be created by making the lines of your linework thicker.

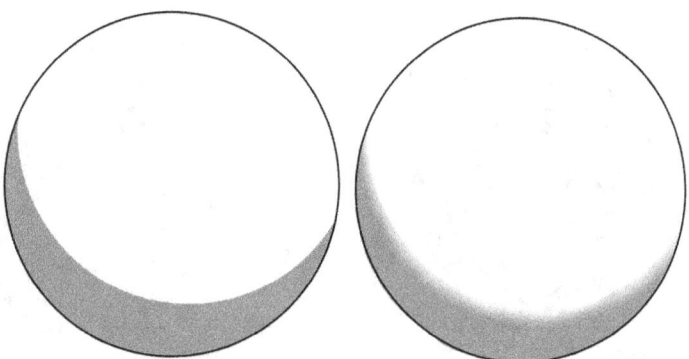

Shading Placement

The placement of your shading is just as important as your technique. Shading the wrong spot can ruin your artwork. When placing shading, the most important thing to do is establish from where your light is coming. Once you've established your light source, identify any part of the body that protrudes or is in front of other parts of the body. These parts will create a shadow in the opposite direction of your light source.

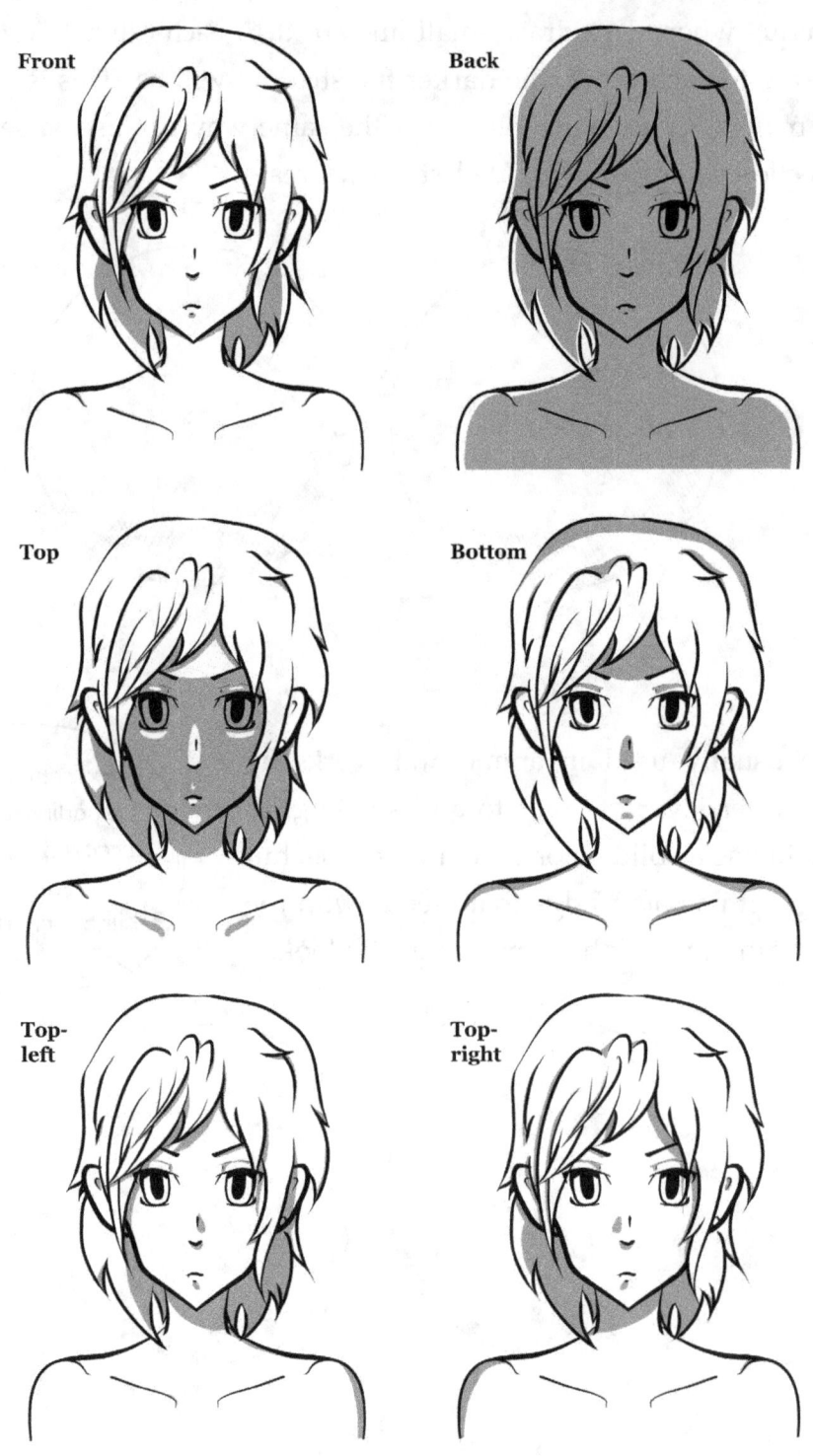

Choosing Colors

Color can be a great tool to develop your art and give depth to your character. Not only does color look good, but it can also help give an idea of your character's likes and personality and help show the type of character they are.

You need to be careful when choosing colors, as not all colors work well together. If you choose the wrong colors, you can also ruin a certain mood you might be trying to create with your character. It's important to understand a little bit about different types of colors and color combinations and how colors affect the mind to choose the best ones for your character.

The Color Wheel

All the colors can be represented in a single color wheel and are divided into one of three groups:

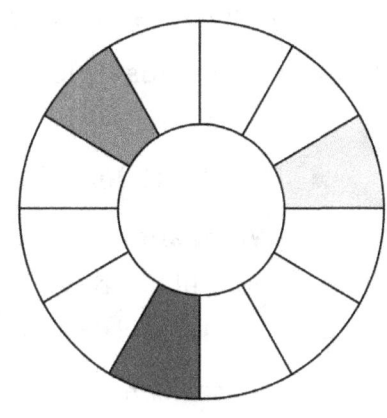

1. **Primary Colors:** These colors are red, yellow, and blue. These three are the most basic colors available and form the building blocks of all other colors.

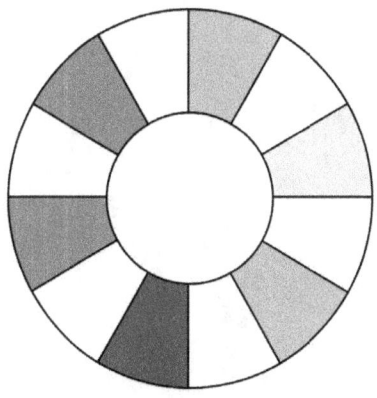

2. **Secondary Colors:** These colors are purple, orange, and green and are created by mixing two primary colors.

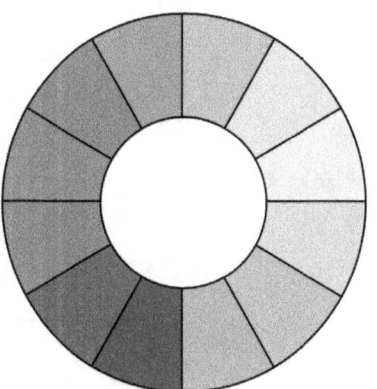

3. **Tertiary Colors:** These are the rest of the colors on the color wheel and are created by mixing a secondary color and a primary color.

Every color imaginable can be created by mixing different amounts of primary, secondary, and tertiary colors.

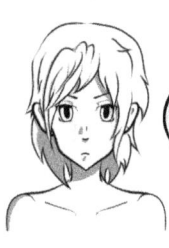

White or black can be added to make a color lighter or darker. If you add white and black, the color will become grayer.

Color Combinations

There are many different ways to combine colors that work well together, most of which are based on the color wheel.

- **Monochromatic:** This simply refers to using different variations of the same color.
- **Complementary Colors:** This type of color combination uses a primary color and the secondary color opposite to the former on the color wheel. These colors can be considered opposites and thus complement each other through their contrast.
- **Split Complementary Colors:** In this combination, you choose a base color and add the two colors on either side of the color on the opposite side of the color wheel.
- **Analogous Colors:** In this color combination, three colors next to each other on the color wheel are used.
- **Triadic Colors:** This system uses three colors that form a triangle on the color wheel.
- **Warm and Cool Colors:** This refers to a combination of colors that create either a 'warm' look, like red, yellow, orange, and green, or colors that create a 'cool' feeling, like blue, purple, and turquoise.

There are *many* other types of color combinations, but these are the basics and a good way to start.

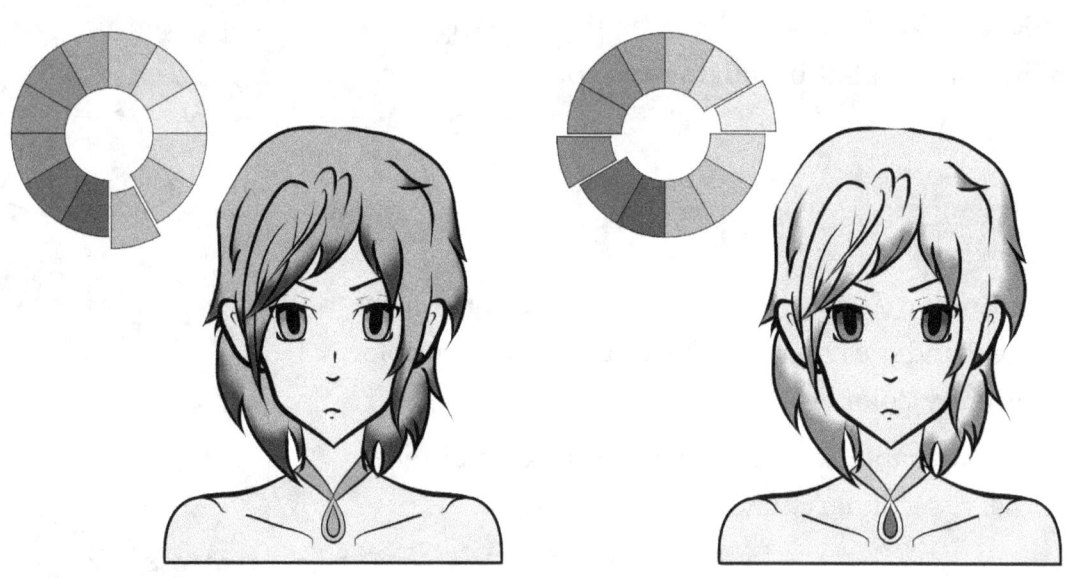

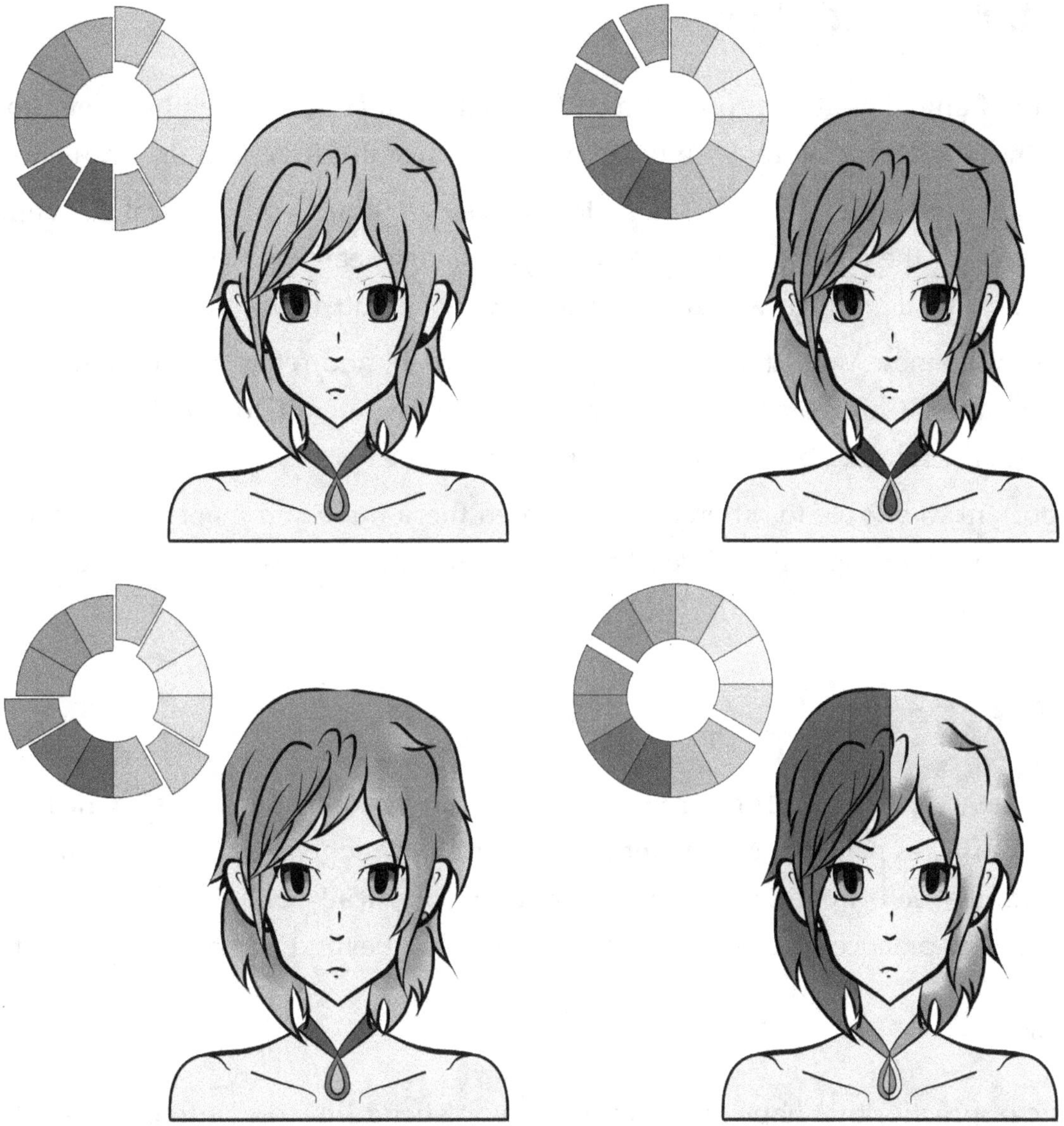

Color Psychology

This doesn't have to be as complicated as it may seem. The mind naturally associates different colors with specific moods and other elements, such as red being associated with danger, anger, and love; green being associated with nature, life, and healing; or yellow being associated with sunshine and positivity. You can use this to your advantage and let the colors tell people a little more about your character. As an example, you can use red as a prominent color to show that

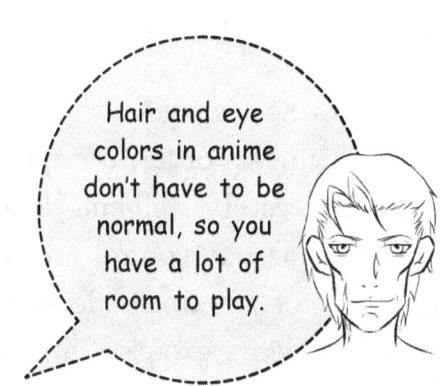

Hair and eye colors in anime don't have to be normal, so you have a lot of room to play.

your character is dangerous or has a temper, or you can use yellow to show that your character is warm and bubbly.

Anime, Manga, and Chibi

If you're a fan of anime, you've probably heard the terms 'manga' and 'chibi' a few times. Many people treat these as the same thing, but there are significant differences that you should know.

'Anime' refers specifically to the animated series or movies you can watch, while 'manga' refers specifically to the comics you can read. If you image-search 'anime', you will find mostly full-color images, while manga will result in mostly black and white linework images.

'Chibi' is a Japanese word that means 'short' or 'small' and refers to an anime style usually directed at children. Chibi characters are most commonly identified by their softer, rounded edges, their small, childlike bodies, and unusually large heads.

It's important to be able to differentiate between these three and incorporate them into your artwork according to the specifics of your characters and the purpose for which these characters have been created.

Always Practice

The Japanese have a proverb: "Tomorrow's battle is won by today's practice", which, in essence, means "practice makes perfect". No matter how much knowledge and theory you have crammed into your head, it won't do you any good if you don't physically practice these skills. There are three basic types of practice that can be applied to any skill beyond just drawing and creating art.

Innate Practice

This is a type of practice that happens naturally as you spend time on your artwork. This focuses on quantity rather than quality, and as long as you spend a little bit each day drawing something, your basic skills will improve over time.

Developmental Practice

This happens when you focus specifically on practicing in order to improve your skills. This can be dull and tedious, but it's the easiest to control and manage. This type of practice is done by doing certain drawing exercises and working on specific skills. The more time you spend on developmental practice every day, the more you will improve.

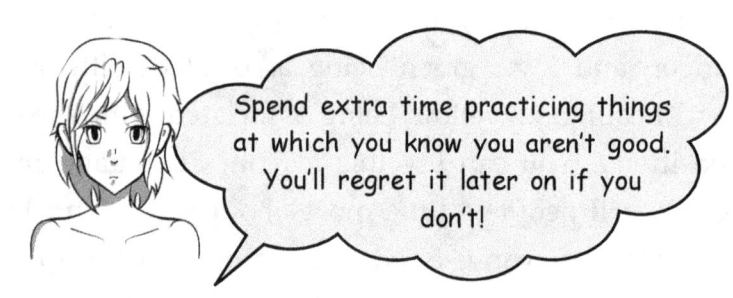

Spend extra time practicing things at which you know you aren't good. You'll regret it later on if you don't!

Inspirational Practice

This is when you experience a sudden burst of improvement after you've been inspired to learn a new skill or create artwork. This type of inspiration depends mainly on your emotions and current frame of mind, so it can't be forced, but it can be encouraged! You can encourage inspiration by surrounding yourself with things that might embolden you to create and learn, like art on your wall, a great workspace, new drawing tools with which to experiment, or "How To" books on any subject that catches your interest. You can also spend time on activities that might inspire you, like going to a museum, looking at work from your favorite artist, or watching an anime with an interesting or strange art style. You should always be prepared for the moments when inspiration strikes by constantly having a pen and a few pieces of paper nearby.

Practice doesn't have to be a time-consuming chore that does nothing but numb the mind. You can do small, simple drawing exercises or make doodles anywhere you have a minute or two to spare, like when you're out taking your pet for a walk or waiting in the dentist's office.

3 School Girls

Now that you've learned the basics, it's finally time to start designing your characters! An excellent way to make great artwork is to think of the drawing you're creating as a 'character' and not as a bunch of lines on paper. Being emotionally invested in your character will be a lot easier to put in the effort and bring more depth and realism to them.

A vast amount of anime will feature a schoolgirl at some point or another, even if she's just passing by in the background. The 'schoolgirl' is one of the most common character-types in anime, making this a great start. In this chapter, we'll be looking at the different elements of drawing this type of character and putting them all together for the final result.

Drawing the Body

Drawing the body is the first step in creating your characters, and it's essential to understand how the female figure works for this.

1. Draw lines to map out the position of the body. Use circles to place all the joints and basic shapes for the head, feet, and hands.

2. Use wedged shapes to draw the base of the torso and hips. The torso uses a more rectangular shape with curved edges, while the hips have a more triangular shape. In the female figure, the hips are slightly wider than the shoulders.

3. Fill up the rest of the body and make sure all the proportions are correct. The head fits into the entire body roughly 6.5 times, the knee is nearly in the middle of the legs, and the wrist is on roughly the same level as the point where the hip and leg meet. Because this type of character is still developing, their hourglass figure isn't too prominent yet, and their chest is still fairly small.

4. Refine the outline of the body, and add details.

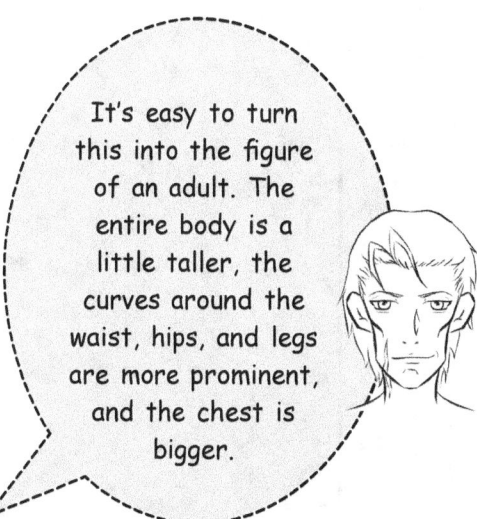

It's easy to turn this into the figure of an adult. The entire body is a little taller, the curves around the waist, hips, and legs are more prominent, and the chest is bigger.

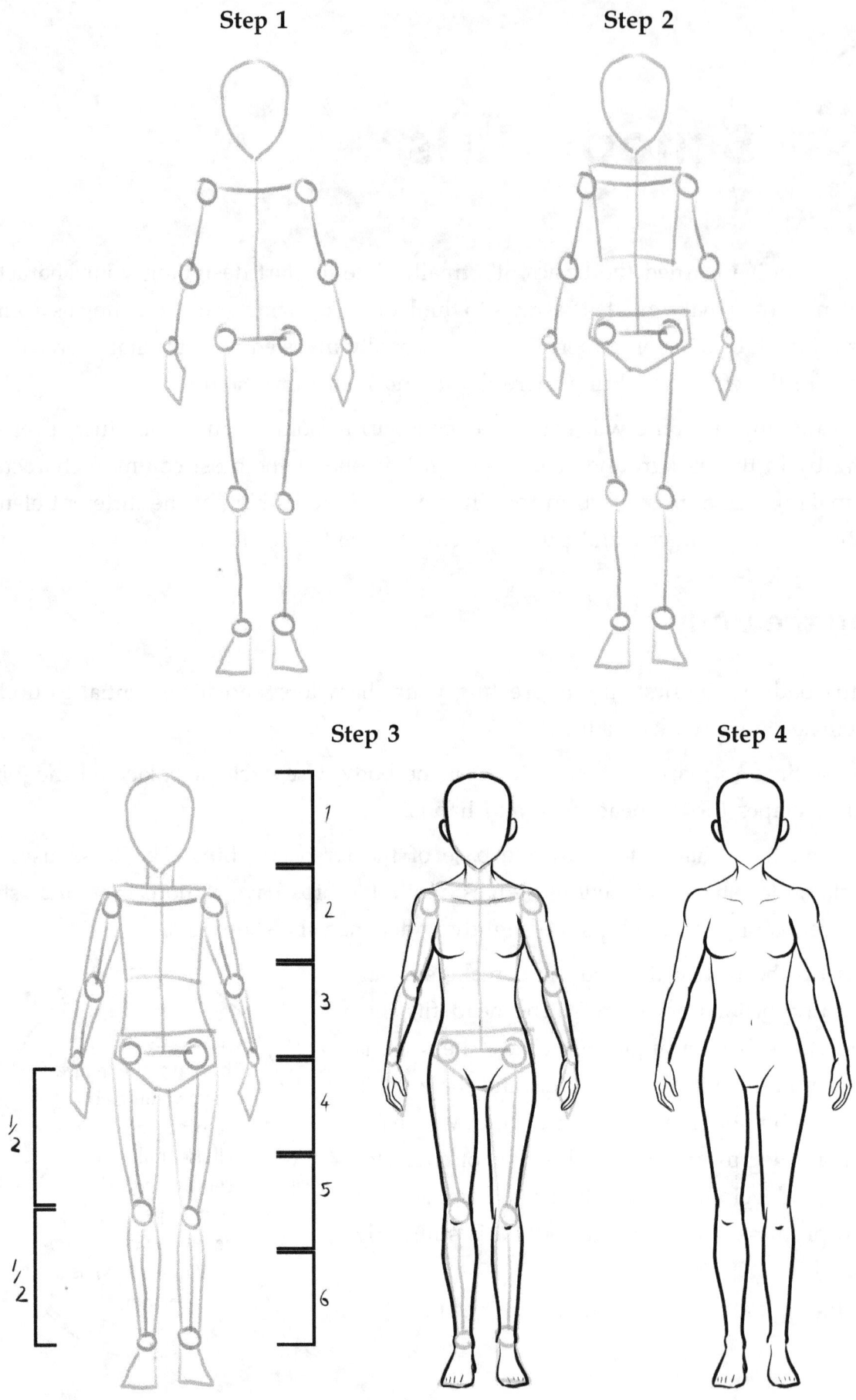

Step 1

Step 2

Step 3

1

2

3

4

5

6

1/2

1/2

Step 4

Drawing the Body

Drawing Eyes

One of the *best* ways to identify the gender of a character from only the face is through the shape of the eyes. Female characters usually have larger, more rounded eyes than male characters.

1. Draw the basic shape of the eye. This will also become the base of the eyelashes.

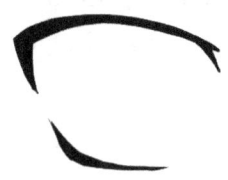 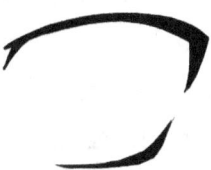

2. Draw a stretched oval to create the iris. The top and bottom of the iris are hidden behind the lids of the eye.

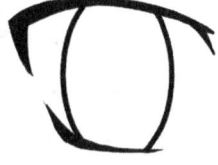 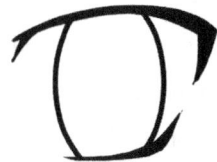

3. Draw in the pupil with the same shape as the iris.

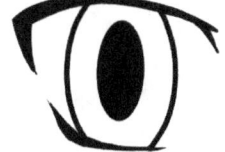 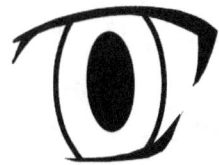

4. Place the reflection spots along the edge of the pupil.

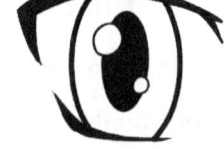 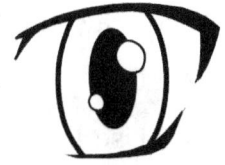

5. Add a shadow to the top of the iris, following the line of the eyelid.

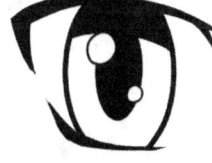 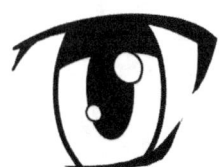

6. Add details, like the fold of the eyelids above the eye, the eyebrows, and the eyelashes.

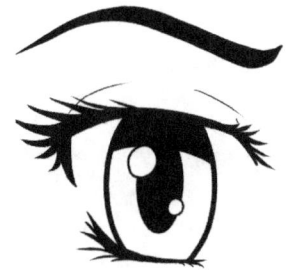 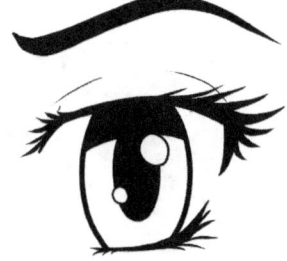

Adding Clothes

Now that your character has a body, it's time to dress them. Drawing clothing is a very simple process. Start by sketching the basic shape of the clothes, then add details like buttons, embellishments, folds, etc. Pay attention to the type of fabric from which the clothes are made. Like those used for a jacket or jersey, some types are thicker and stiffer, meaning they slightly conceal the silhouette and cause a few larger folds, while others, like those used for the shirt, are softer and cling to the body. It would help if you also considered how tight and form-fitting the clothing article should usually be. Lastly, you should pay attention to layers and how they affect each other. It's a good idea to start with the base layer of clothes and cover it with the next layer, just like when you're *actually* getting dressed.

Because most anime are set in Japan, the schoolgirl character will usually spend most of her time wearing a school uniform or wearing the uniform of her club activities. You will usually find one of three typical uniform types: the basic shirt and pants/skirt accompanied by a jersey or bolo jacket, the iconic sailor uniform, or the high-collared gakuran. You may want to spend a little time researching these uniforms to help give you a better idea of how to clothe your character.

Skirts

The skirt can be a little tricky to manage, but here is a simple guide to help you:

1. Draw the basic shape of the front of the skirt onto your body.
2. Draw the band around the waist and any visible parts of the back of the skirt.
3. Use lines to place folds or pleats.
4. Shape the hem of the skirt according to your fold lines, and add details.

Step 1	Step 2	Step 3

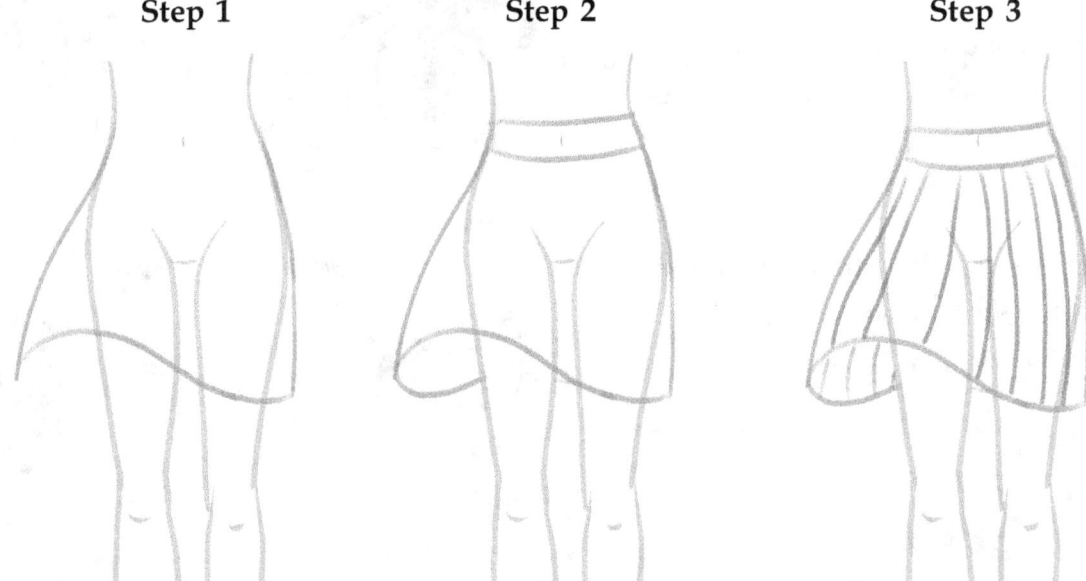

Step 4

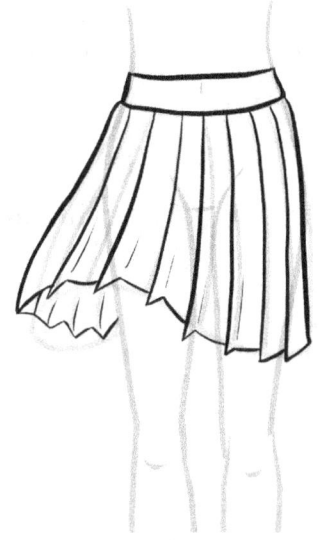
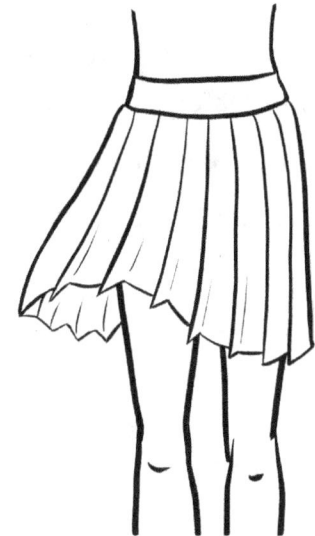

Shading Hair

You know how to draw hair, but now it's time to learn shading.

1. Start by adding a base color.

2. Use a darker shade of the same color to add shadow areas. These are all further away from the light source, like the tips curling towards the face, sections behind other strands, and the hair beneath the head and behind the neck.

   You can put in the highlights either by erasing the color or adding white with correction fluid, paint, or ink.

3. Add highlights to the widest areas around the head and on areas that are especially close to the lightsource. These highlights should be created using varying small, vertical lines that follow the flow of the hair.

Step 1

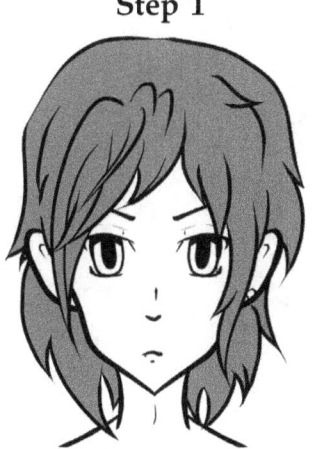

Step 2

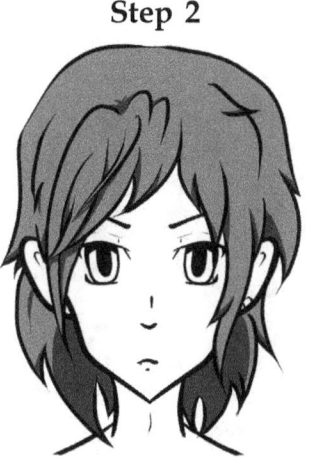

Step 3

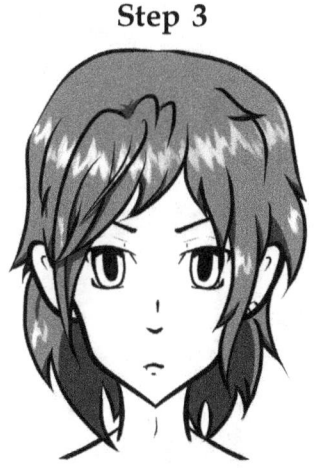

Putting It All Together

Now that you've learned about the different aspects of this type of character, it's finally time to put everything together and create your schoolgirl.

1. Follow the steps above and draw the body.

2. Draw in the face and hands. Add any objects with which your character might be holding or interacting.

3. Add the clothing and hair.

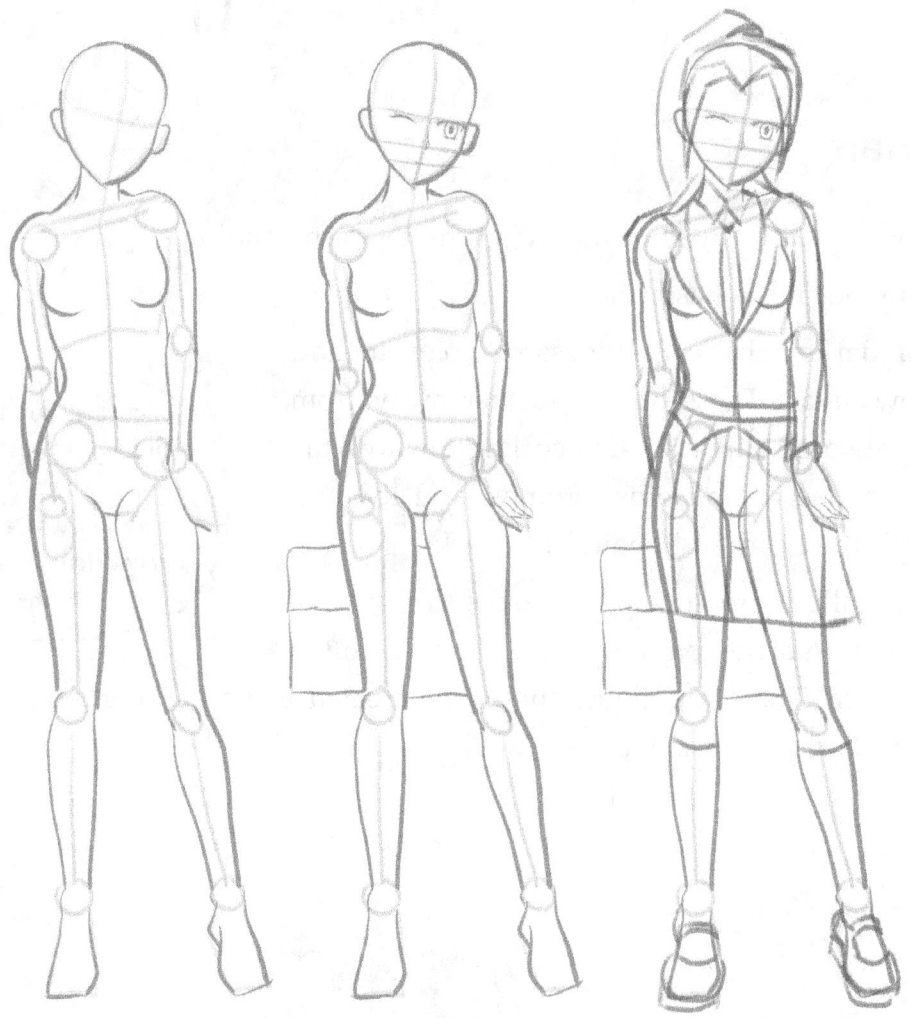

4. Add final details.

5. Strengthen the drawing, and erase unnecessary lines that may distract you.

6. Ink your final linework.

7. Add color and shading to finish your design.

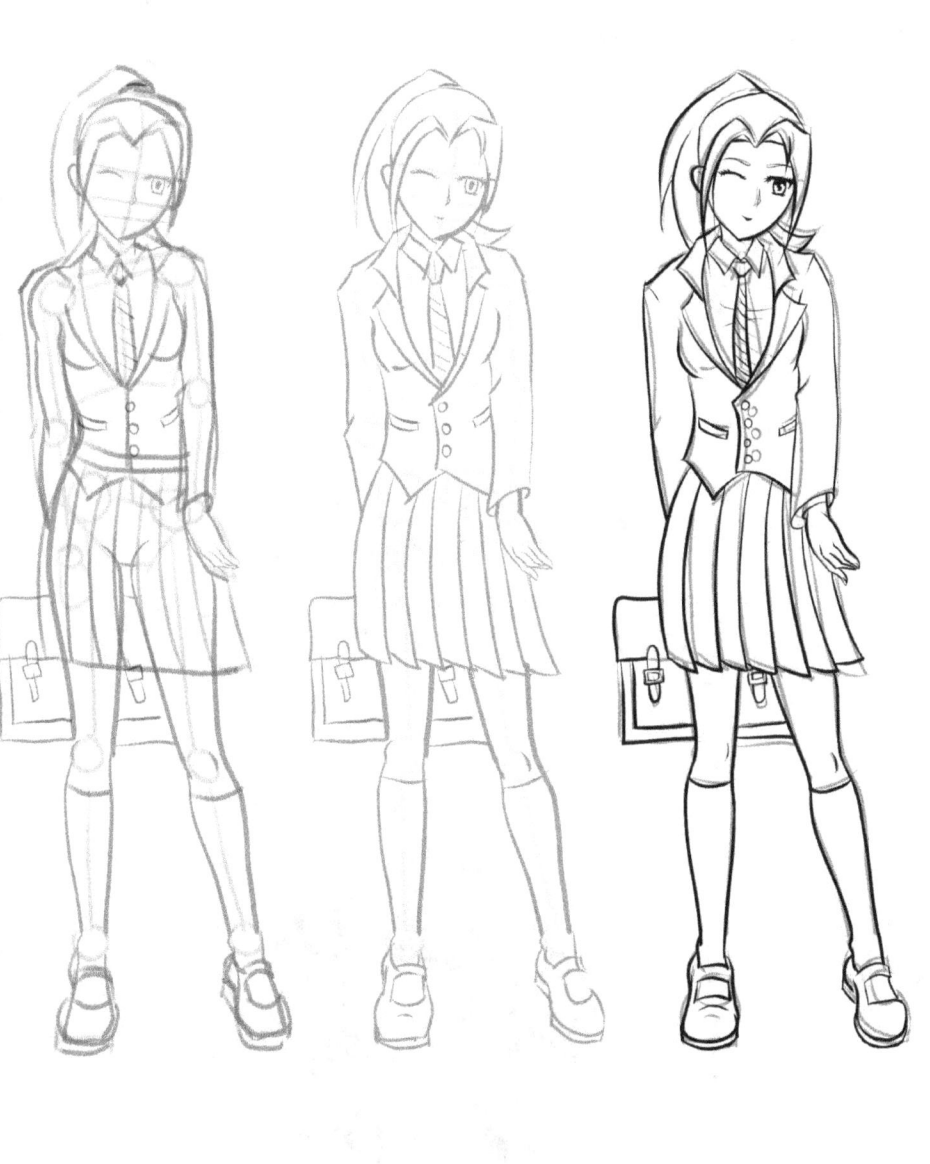

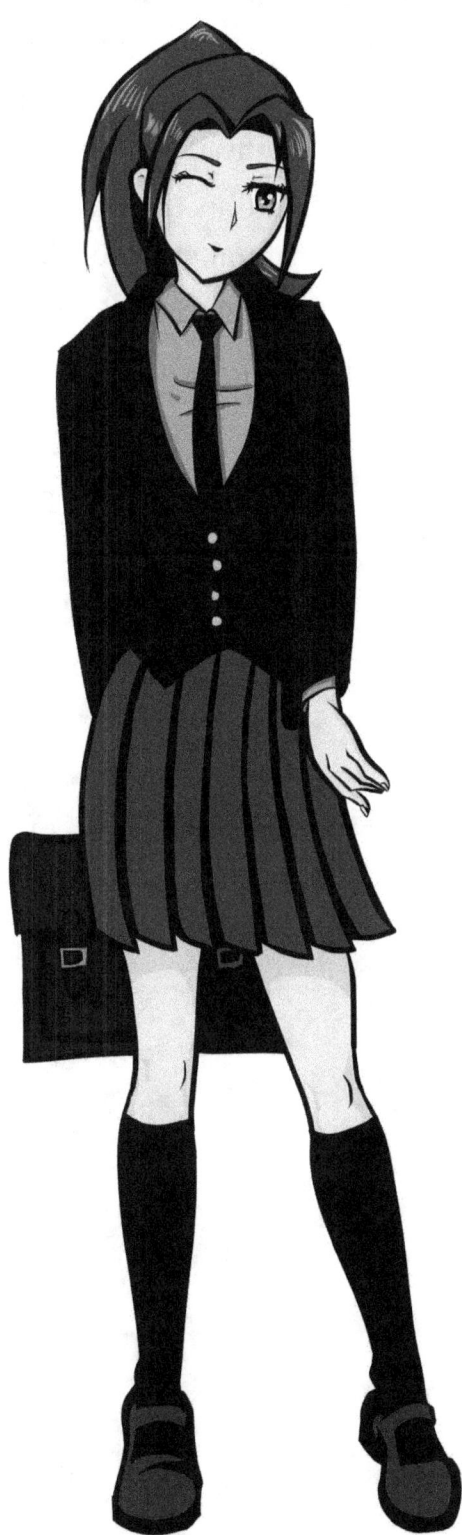

The Cat Girl

This is a little bonus to add a touch of whimsy and fantasy to your character. It has become quite popular to incorporate a cat girl into an anime somewhere in the plot, and many fans seem to love it; so, here is a guide on how to give your school girl some cute cat ears.

1. Once you have the basic shape of your head and hair, draw two triangles to the top of the head on either side.

2. Add another line inside the ears to indicate the natural shape of the ear.

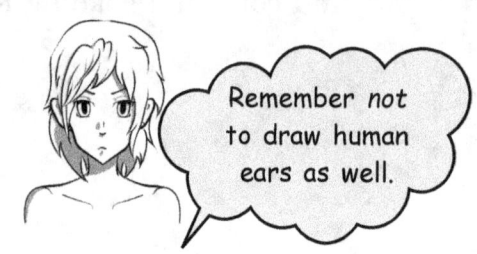

Remember *not* to draw human ears as well.

3. Add details such as ear-fluff and tufts at the tips.

4. Alter the hair to flow around the ears so that they look more natural.

Step 1

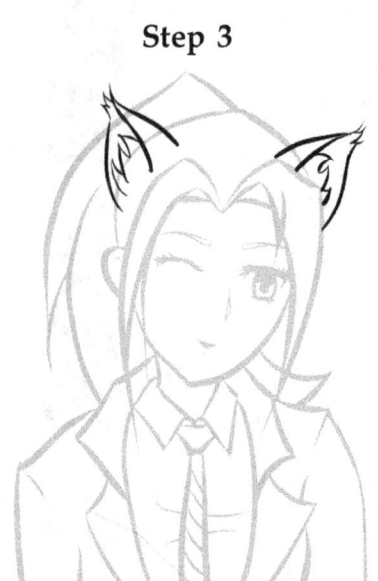

Step 2

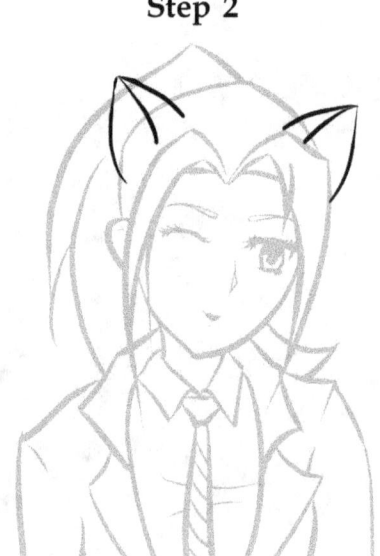

Step 3

Step 4

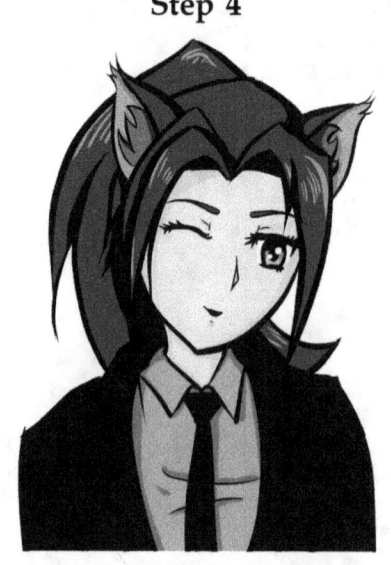

Schoolboys

If your anime has a schoolgirl, it will most likely have a school*boy* as well. Drawing this next character is a great way to learn the differences between male and female characters.

The Body

Drawing the male body is just as simple as drawing the female body. Still, there are some significant differences of which you need to be aware so that even if your characters are relatively young and at the beginning of their development, you can still distinguish between boys and girls.

1. Map the position and pose of the body using lines, circles, and basic shapes.

2. Draw in the torso and hips. Unlike women, the shoulders are the widest part of the body, and the hips are about the same width as the waist.

3. Draw the shape and outline of the body. If your character is still in his very early teens, his chest will be mostly straight, and he will have very little muscle definition. For this example, however, we will use a teen in high school who is a little more developed. The chest is slightly wider than the waist and hips. The arms and legs are a little thicker than those of a woman and they can sometimes have a little more muscle definition. The male neck is also a little thicker.

4. Add details.

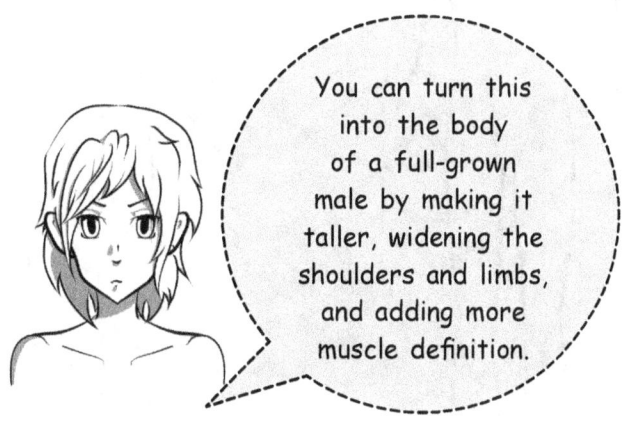

You can turn this into the body of a full-grown male by making it taller, widening the shoulders and limbs, and adding more muscle definition.

Step 1   **Step 2**   **Step 3**

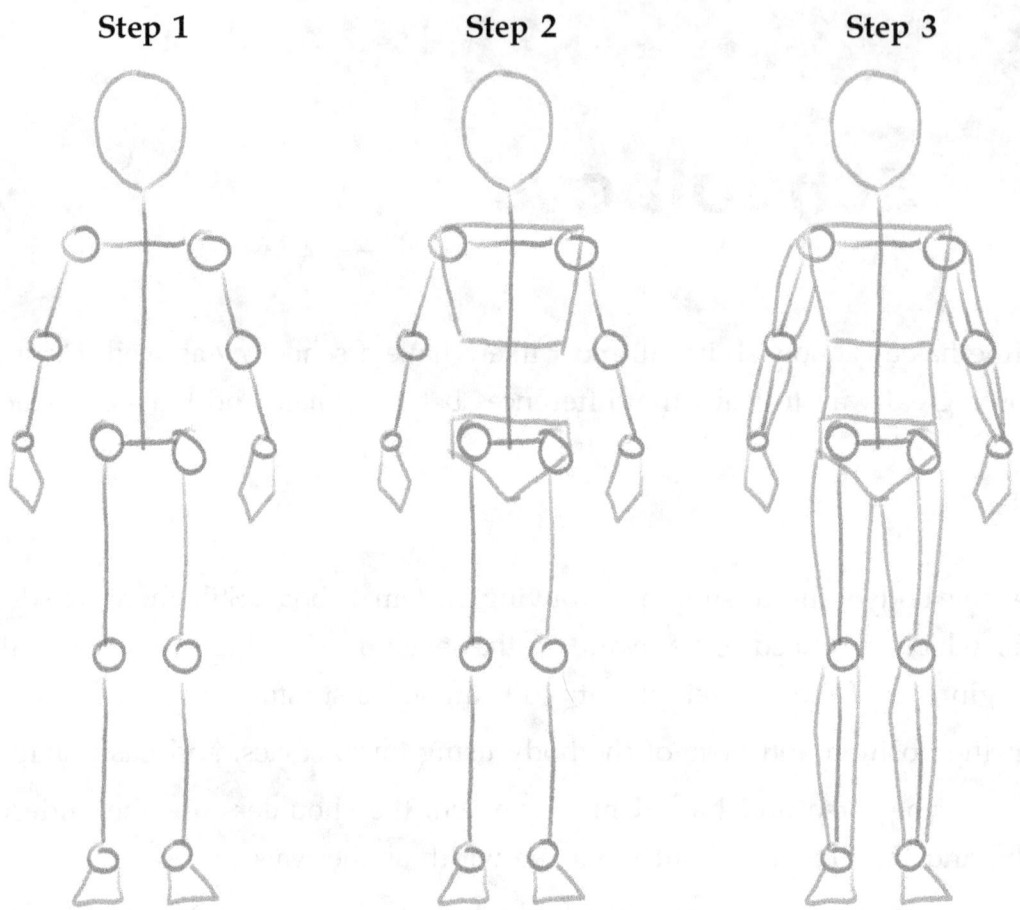

Step 4

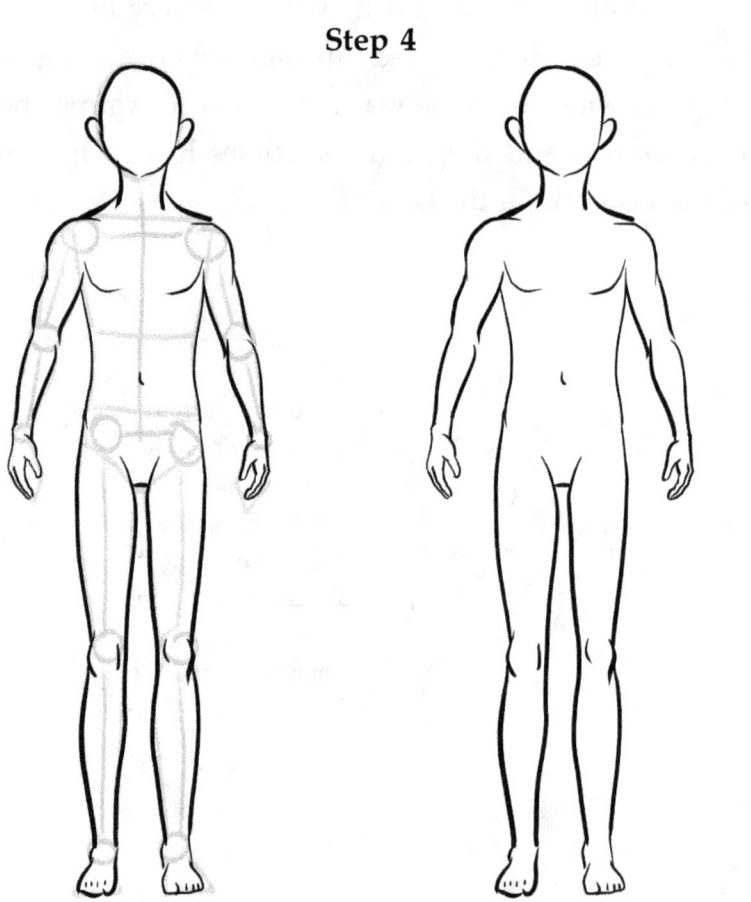

Adding Muscles

This is for when you're drawing the great sports stars and athletes of the school. While regular teenagers don't usually have a lot of bulging, gleaming muscles, those who participate in sports, have a very active lifestyle, or train a lot will have at least some muscles. Some anime will often exaggerate the muscles of certain characters to help portray their role and personality better. Drawing muscles is relatively simple, but it does take some understanding of the human body, especially for the torso.

1. Draw the basic shape of the body. The neck is thicker, the shoulders and chest are wider, and most of the lines in the arms and legs are drawn with an exaggerated curve, making the muscles bulge.

2. Draw a line down the center of the chest to help keep things symmetrical and add the collarbones.

3. Draw in the pectoral muscles on the chest and the vertical lines for the abs.

4. Use horizontal lines to finish the abs, and draw in the shoulder muscle.

5. Add in the details like the muscles along the chest's side and the 'V' lines above the legs.

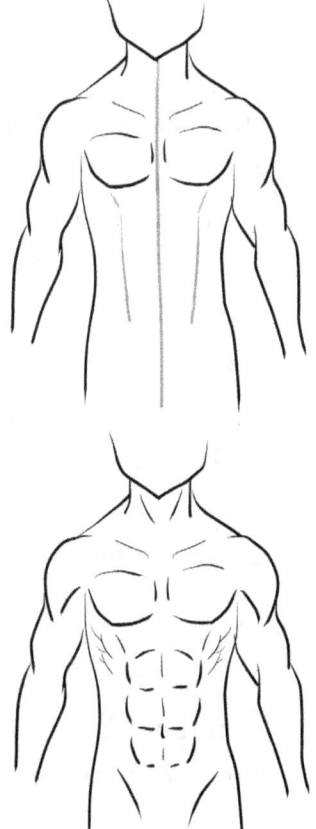

The more intensely you apply these steps and the more details you add, the more your character will look muscled.

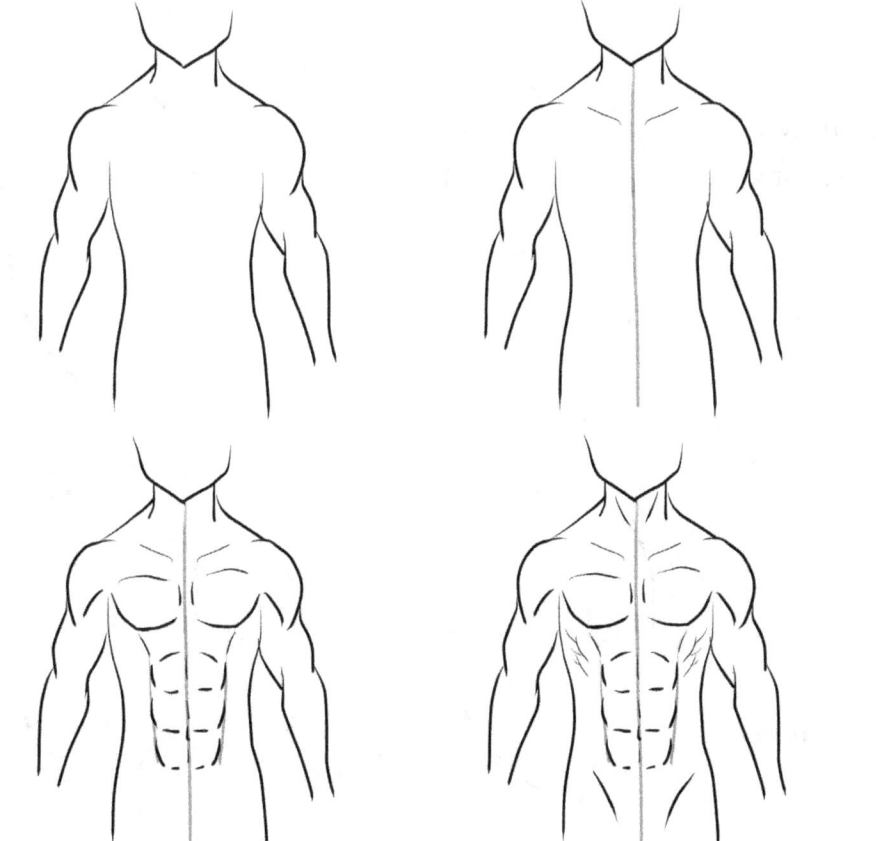

Drawing the Head

In anime, heads tend to be reasonably feminine, so you need to put in a little effort to make your head seem more masculine. While drawing both male and female heads follows the same process, some methods make the naturally feminine head look more masculine.

- The male head is a little longer and narrower than the female head. Young boys and teens, however, have faces slightly shorter than full-grown men.

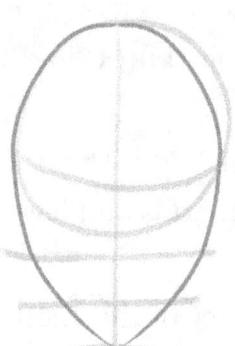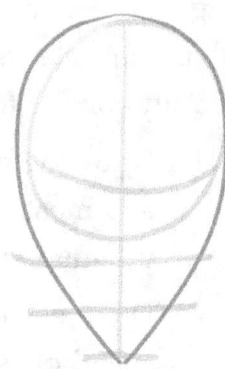

- The neck for men is thicker than for women.

- Men have a more angled face, while women have more rounded faces.

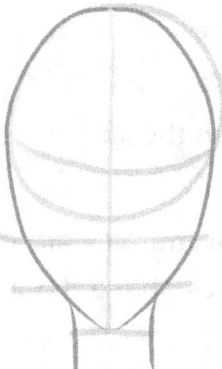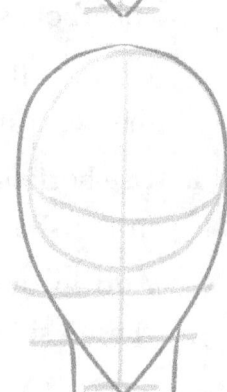

- Men have a more pronounced, sharper jaw. When drawing younger men, like teenagers, the jaw isn't as pronounced, and you need to use softer curves and lines. However, you can still emphasize the jaw by making it a little lower and using a smaller curve when creating the jaw.

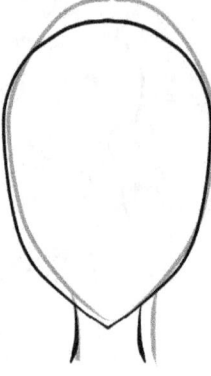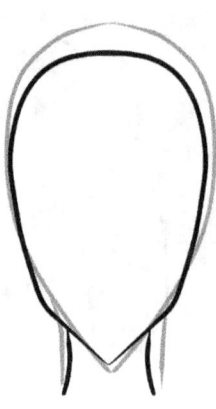

- Men and boys have a more squared hairline.

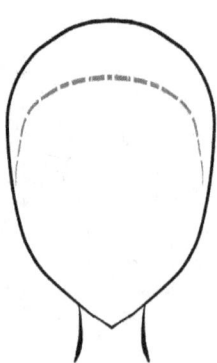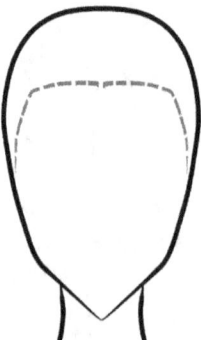

Side Profile

Drawing the head and face in a side profile can be a *bit* more tricky, so let's take a look at some ways to do this easily:

1. Draw a circle, and add the center line on the side of the circle in the direction your character is looking.

2. Add the eye, nose, mouth, and chin-lines as you would for a frontal view.

3. Draw the basic shape of the face. The face dips inward from the center line towards the middle of the mouth and then outward again to form the nose. Turn back in again just above the nose and draw a straight line towards the chin-line. Curve the line inward in a diagonal line. This line goes to roughly the middle of the circle on the mouth-line. Turn upward to make the jaw.

4. To draw the nose and mouth, use the line from the tip of the nose to the chin as a guide. The nose dips in so that the bottom of the nose is on the nose-line. Then, the face dips out again for the mouth. The lips protrude out again, with the bottom lip ending on the mouth-line. The face then goes out again to create the chin.

5. Draw the eye, and place the ear. The ear starts in the last third of the circle between the eye and nose-line. Remember that the eye should be drawn from a *side* angle.

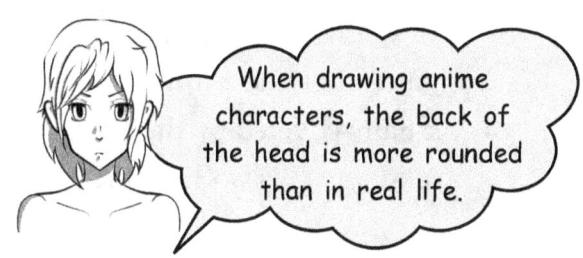

When drawing anime characters, the back of the head is more rounded than in real life.

6. Erase the lines you don't need, and add details.

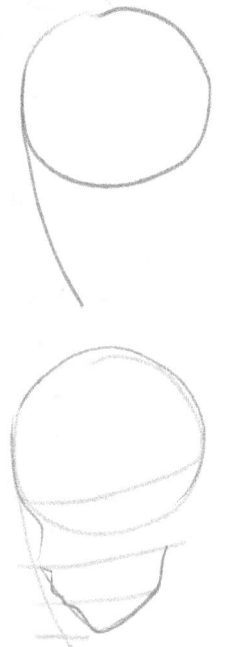
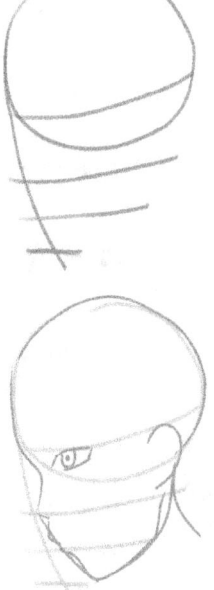
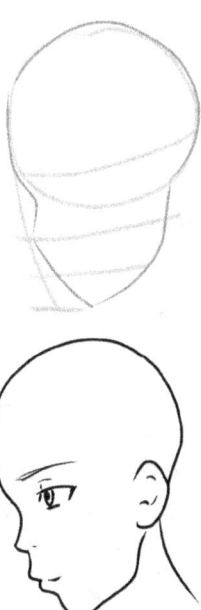

Drawing Male Eyes

Drawing male eyes follows the same process as female eyes, but there are a few differences to make them more masculine:

1. Draw the basic shape of the eye. The upper lid is a little wider and has sharper angles, while the lower lid is a little higher.

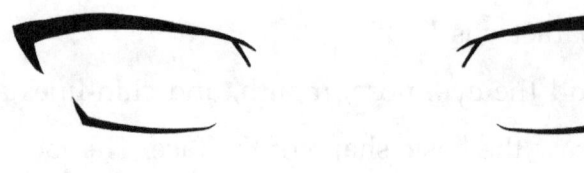

2. Draw in the iris using an oval shape. The upper eyelid usually covers the top of the iris, but the bottom of the iris doesn't touch the lower lid.

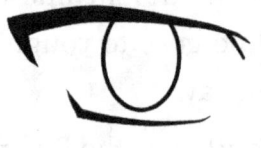 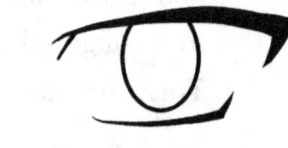

3. Draw in the pupil. There is a chance that the pupil is also partially covered by the upper eyelid, but this isn't a set rule.

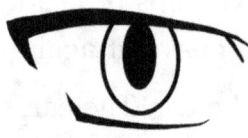 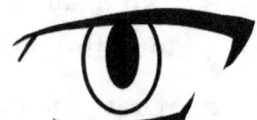

4. Add the reflection spots to the iris and pupil.

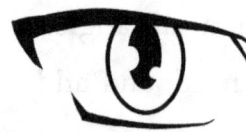 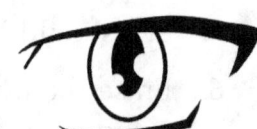

5. Add shading to the top of the iris.

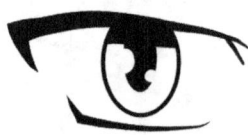 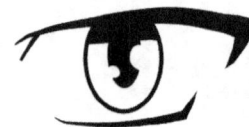

6. Draw in all the details. Remember that male eyes don't have extra eyelashes.

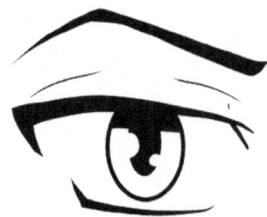 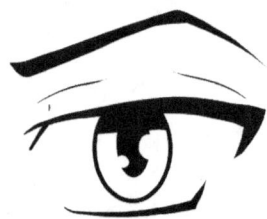

Male eyebrows are sharper than female eyebrows and are drawn using mostly straight lines.

Adding Clothes

The same rules apply to both male and female characters when it comes to adding clothes. Work in layers from the bottom up, and keep in mind how the different types of fabric fold and cling to the body.

The pants and shoes are almost always the same with boys, no matter which type of uniform they wear, so you will have to focus on details regarding the shirt and jacket to help distinguish this uniform from that of another school. You should remember that schools switch out their uniforms as the seasons change, such as a dress shirt and bolo jacket in the winter becoming a polo shirt in the summer.

Lastly, while all the characters in the school will be wearing the same uniform, you can still bring in some individuality through the way they wear their clothes. For example, the student who strives for academic prestige will usually have the most pristine uniform possible, while a delinquent-type character will not put in any effort. His shirt won't be tucked in properly, his collar might be unbuttoned, and his tie will be loose and sloppy. Some characters will also add their own flair by wearing accessories around their arms or neck.

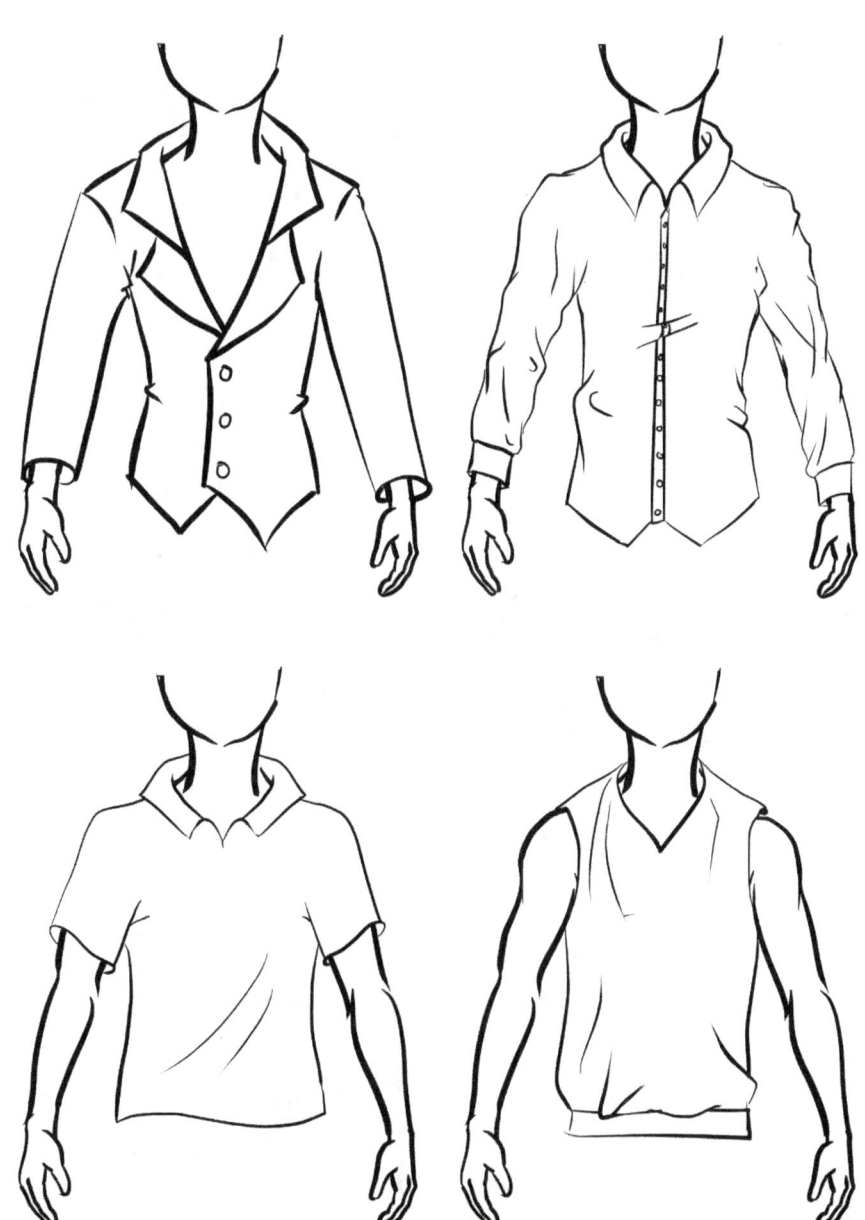

Putting It All Together

Now it's time to bring all these elements together to create your schoolboy.

1.   Draw the body, and add muscles if it applies to the character.

2.   Add the face and hands, as well as anything with which your character may be interacting.

3.   Draw in the clothes and hair.

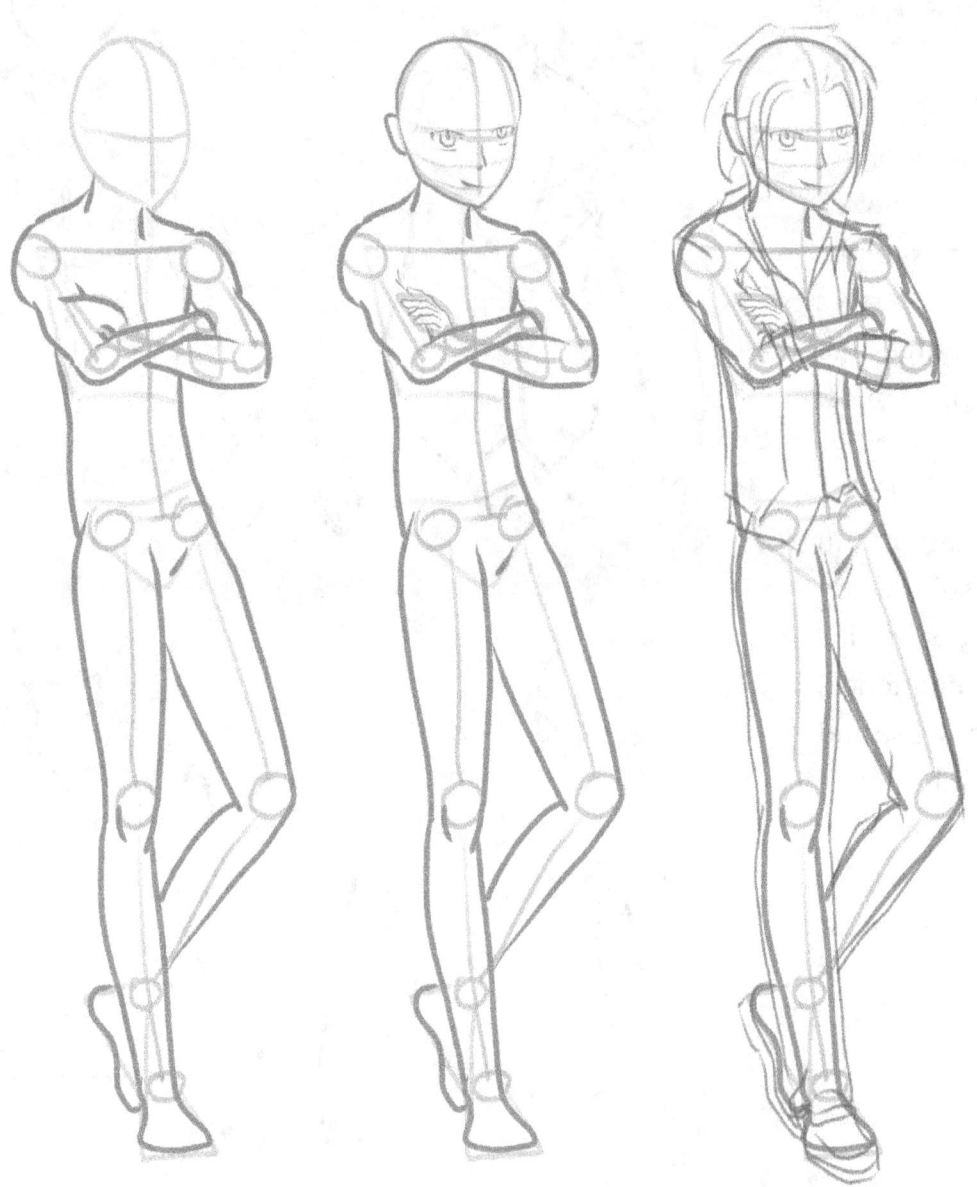

4. Add all your final details.

5. Refine, and clean up your drawing.

6. Ink the linework.

7. Add color and shading.

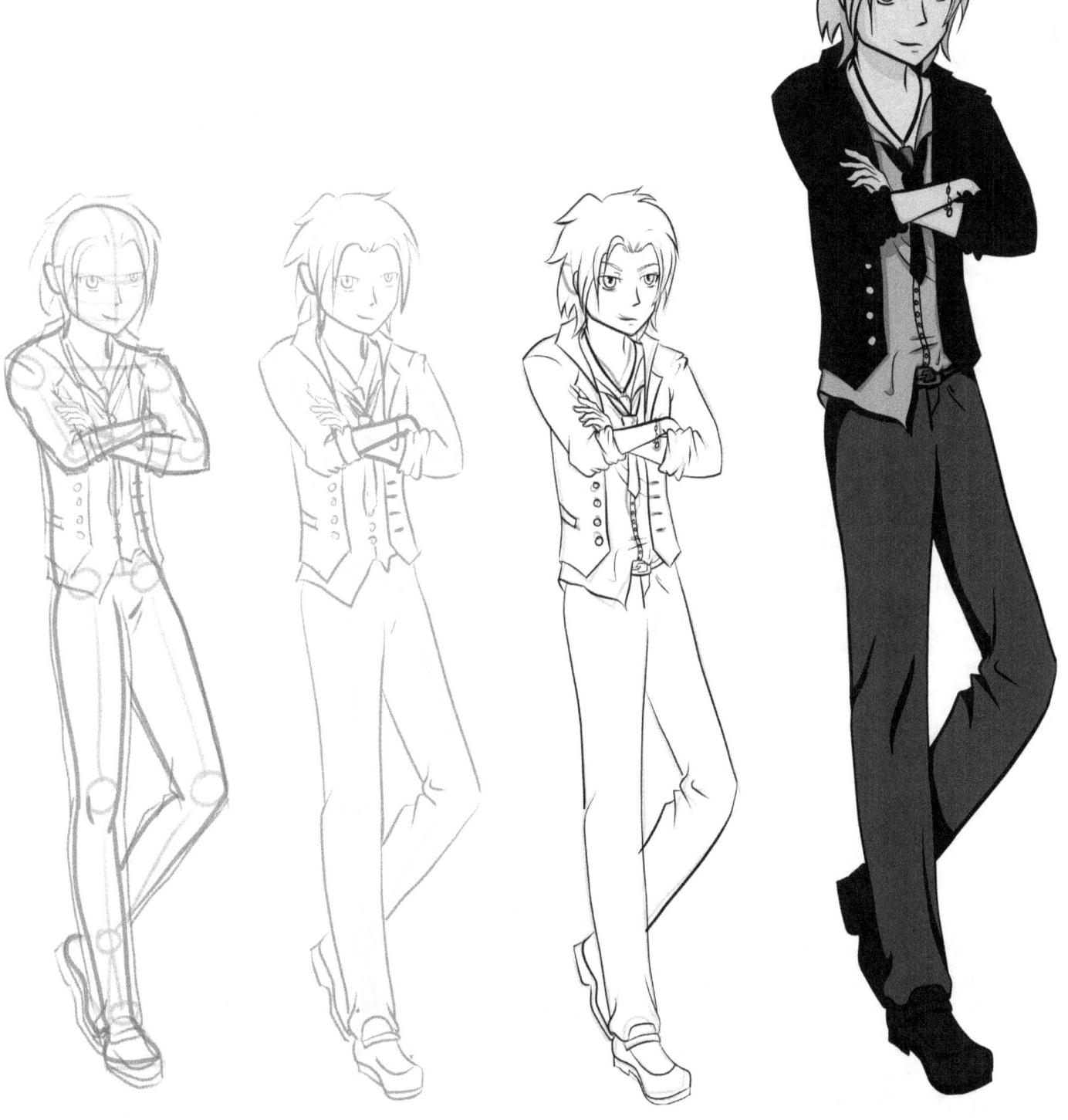

Preteens

Preteens and children are another popular character-type. They can also be a very important addition to your anime or manga, especially if you want to create something with backstories, large families, or something that appeals to a younger demographic.

The Body

Because preteens and children are constantly growing, this is the body-type that has the most variants and proportion sets. It can be a little tricky, and you need to put in some effort to make sure your preteen doesn't end up looking like a young teenager. One of the best things about drawing preteens is that they are usually simplified, and both boys and girls have the same body-type at this stage. We will take a look at all the significant differences as we draw.

1. Draw the basic pose. Preteens are smaller, and depending on their age, their head fits into the body three to five times. The legs meet the hips roughly halfway between the neck and feet. Use very small circles to place the joints.

2. Place the torso and hips. Both the torso and hips use rectangle-like shapes and are the same width. The shoulders are only slightly wider than the torso.

3. Create the outline of your character. Children tend to be bony and have very little shape, so you don't need to use strong curves while drawing the body. The arms and legs are also fairly thin.

4. Add the details. Because they don't have any strong bone structure, the details, such as the collarbones, are quite faint.

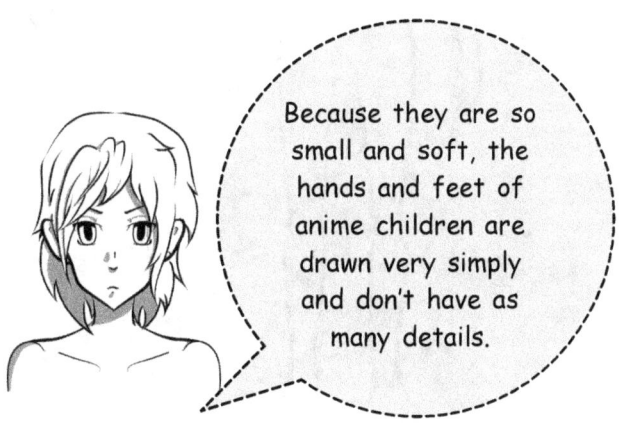

Because they are so small and soft, the hands and feet of anime children are drawn very simply and don't have as many details.

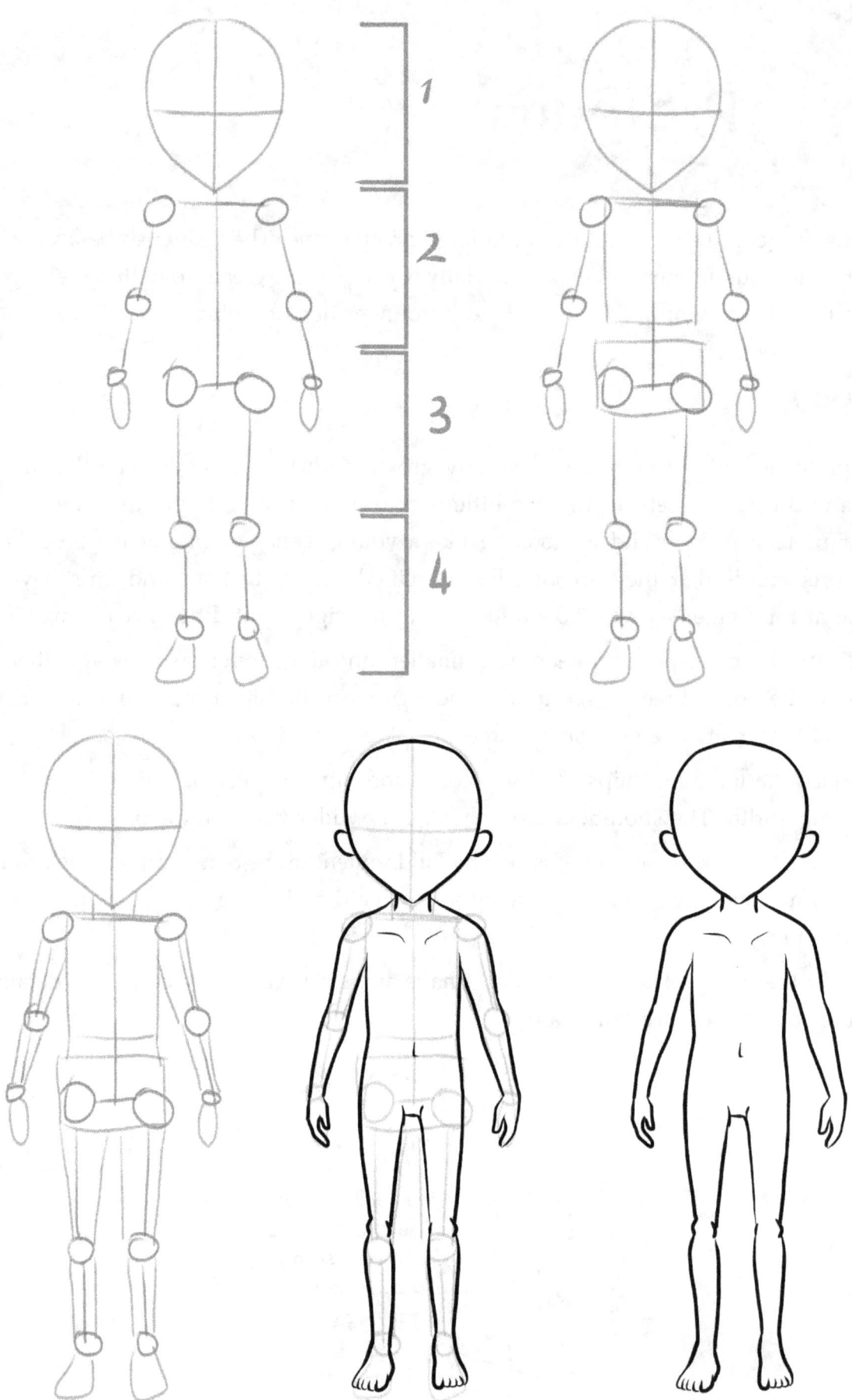

The Head

Like the body, the heads of anime preteens are also different from teens and adults, but the same shape is used for both boys and girls once again. One of the most significant ways to differentiate age in such young characters lies in the hairstyle and eyes.

1. Draw a circle with a center line.

2. Put in the rest of the construction lines. Start with the chin-line. Measure where you would normally place the eye-line and add that short distance below the circle to place the chin-line. The eye-line is exactly in the middle between the chin-line and the top of the circle. The nose and mouth-lines are measured as usual.

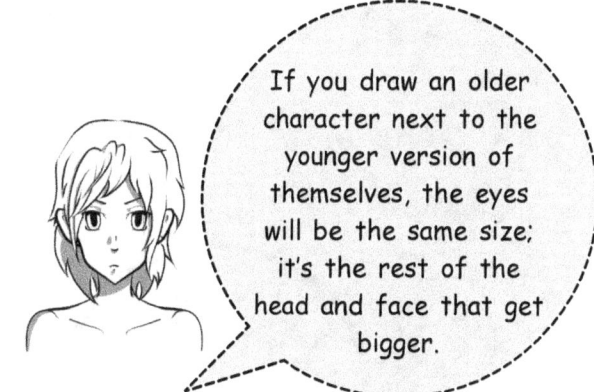

If you draw an older character next to the younger version of themselves, the eyes will be the same size; it's the rest of the head and face that get bigger.

3. Draw the lower half of the face. The jaw and cheeks are fairly wide, while the chin is very short and round.

4. Draw in the eyes. The eyes of preteen characters are very large in relation to the head.

5. Place the nose and mouth. These characters have faces that are a little squished into the bottom of the face, so the mouth, nose, and eyes are quite close together. The nose isn't very prominent, and you should use very small lines to draw it. Some anime leave the nose out completely.

6. Place the ears between the eye and nose-line.

7. Add the details. Most of the details are also fairly faint and small. The eyebrows are also thinner on children and preteens than on adults and teenagers.

Many anime like to use small circles or lines to add a permanent blush on a child's face, especially for little girls.

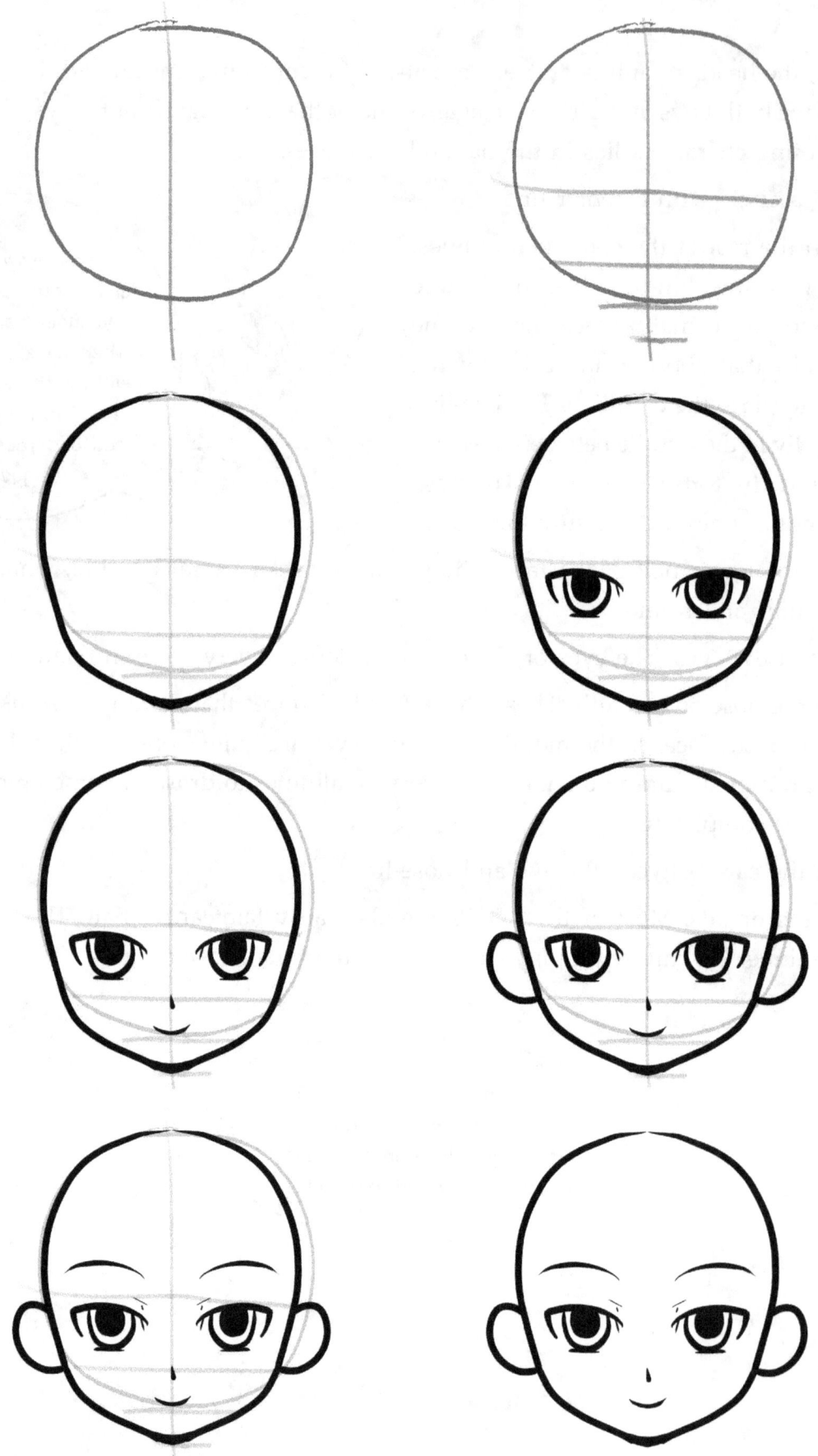

Adding Clothes

Clothing is another great way to help differentiate between a boy and a girl. Take a little time to look at popular clothing styles for boys and girls as a reference.

In most cases, these characters will be wearing clothes that are light, loose, and easy to move in since they love to play and run around. They will also wear very few layers of clothing for the same reason, unless they're bundled up for winter. Children's clothing also tends to be on the simpler side to help portray the innocence and simplicity of their youth. It's quite common for young boys in anime to wear shorts rather than long pants, and girls usually wear a type of dress. Puffed sleeves and collars on dresses are especially popular for young anime girls. Unless your preteen is in a formal setting, such as going to school or attending an important event, they will most likely be barefoot.

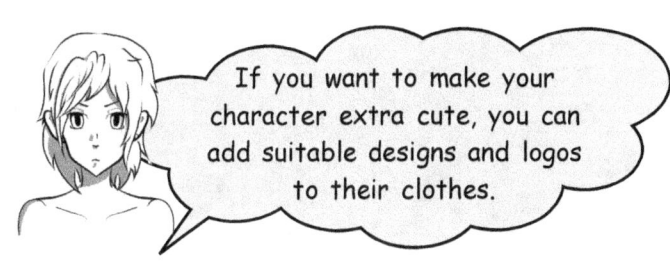

If you want to make your character extra cute, you can add suitable designs and logos to their clothes.

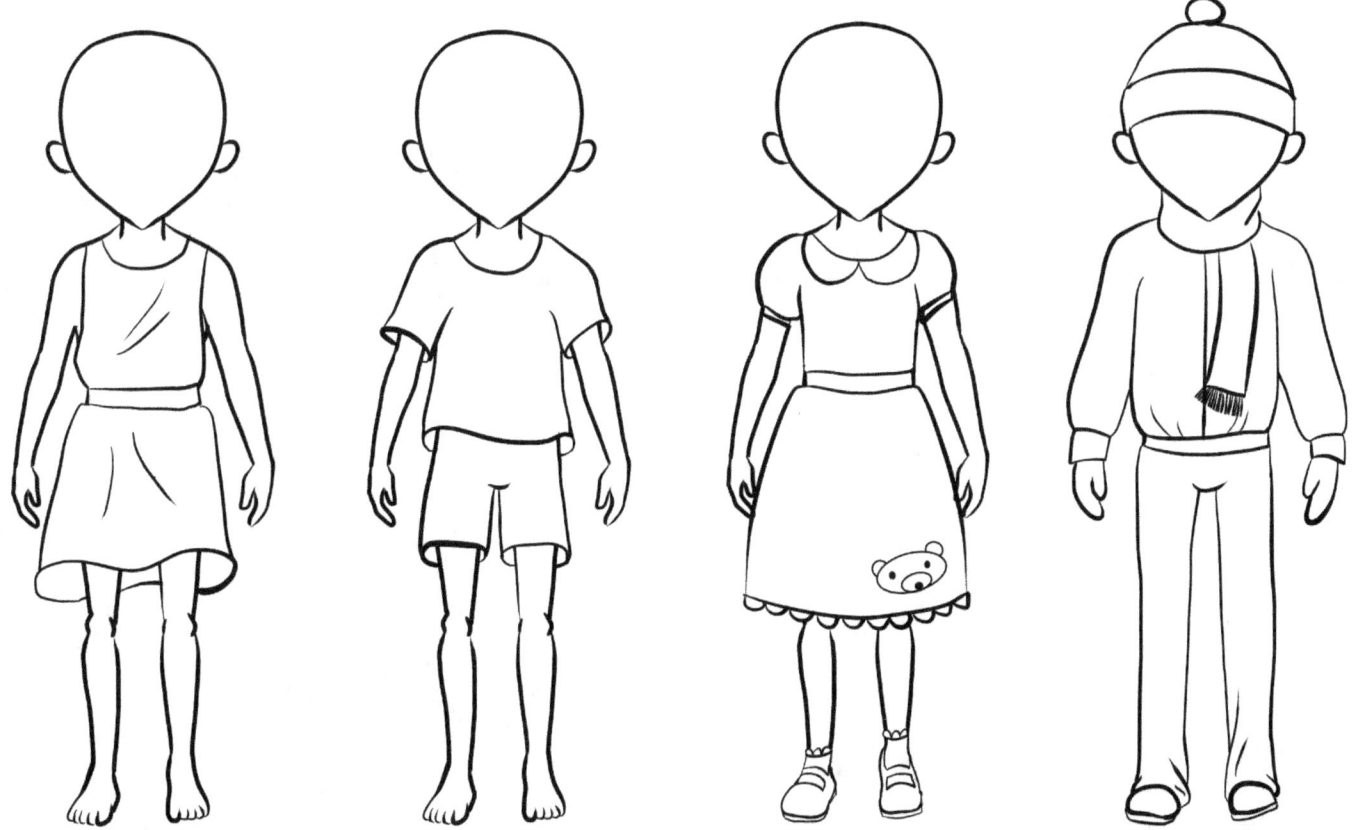

Putting It All Together

Now it's time to take everything we've covered here and turn it into a supercute kid.

1. Map out the basic pose. Remember to adjust your proportions according to age and find a pose that is typical of this type of character.
2. Draw the outline of the body.

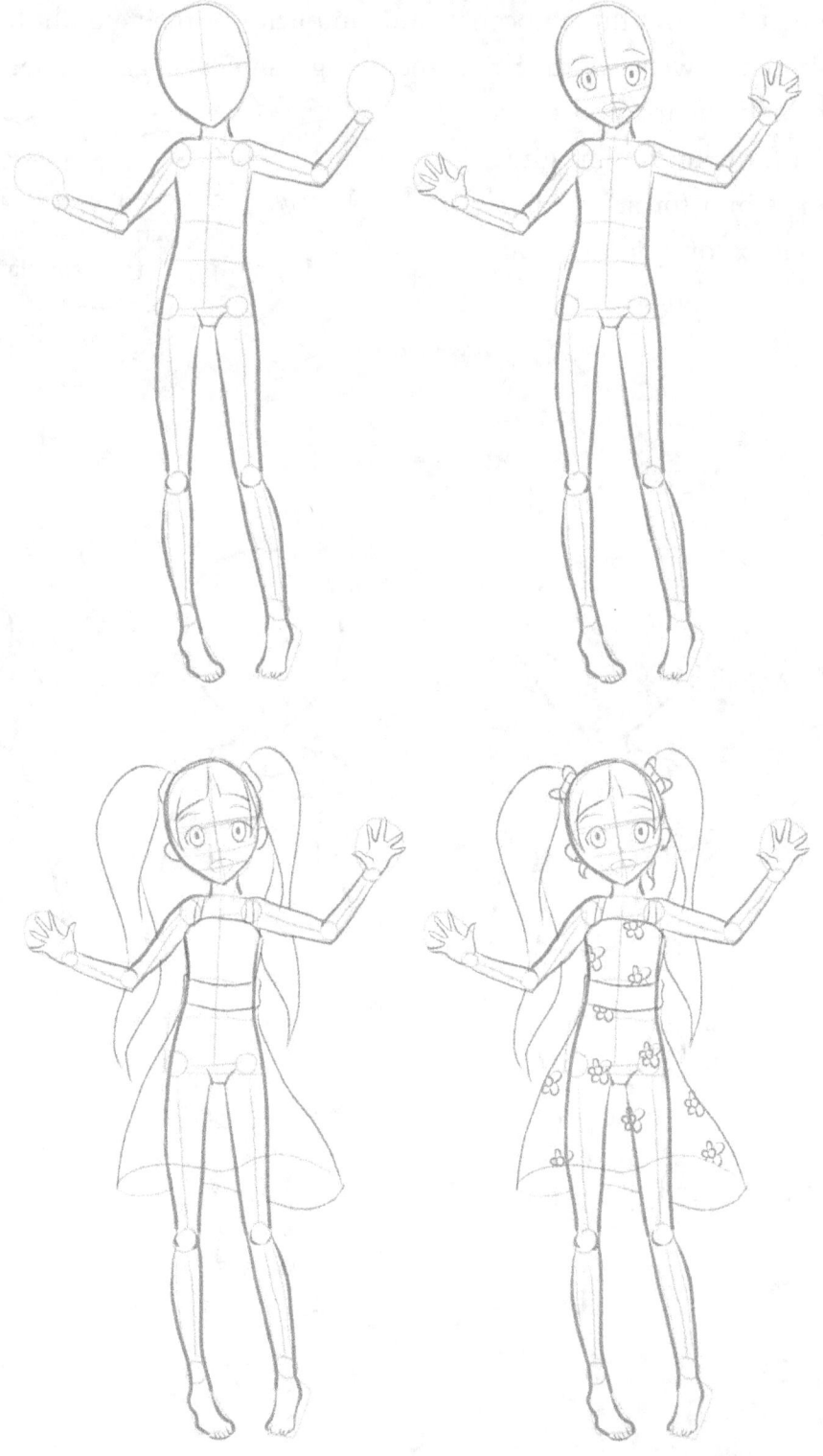

3. Add the face and hands (and the feet if they're barefoot).

4. Add the clothing and hair.

5. Draw in the final details, and clean up the drawing.

6. Ink your linework.

7. Add color and shading.

Choosing colors for children works the same way as choosing colors for older characters, but keep in mind that children will usually lean towards bright, playful colors when given a choice. Parents, however, often like to dress their children in more pastel colors and tend to stick to gender stereotypes, like pink and purple for girls and blue and green for boys.

The Vampire Girl

A type of character that manga and artists all over the world like to draw now and then is the "vampire girl". This is a way to take something usually considered dangerous and turn it into something cute or to put a little edge onto something innocent and sweet. Most of the changes for this center around the head and face, so here is a bonus guide on how to turn your sweet little girl into the most adorable little monster ever:

1. Begin with the outline of the head.

2. Draw the eyes. For a vampire girl, the eyes are a little bit closer together. The upper eyelid is drawn slanting down towards the center, while the outer edge is drawn with sharp lines. The iris and pupil are smaller than usual, and the lower lid is a little higher to make the eye narrower. All of this gives her a slightly more dangerous and aggressive look.

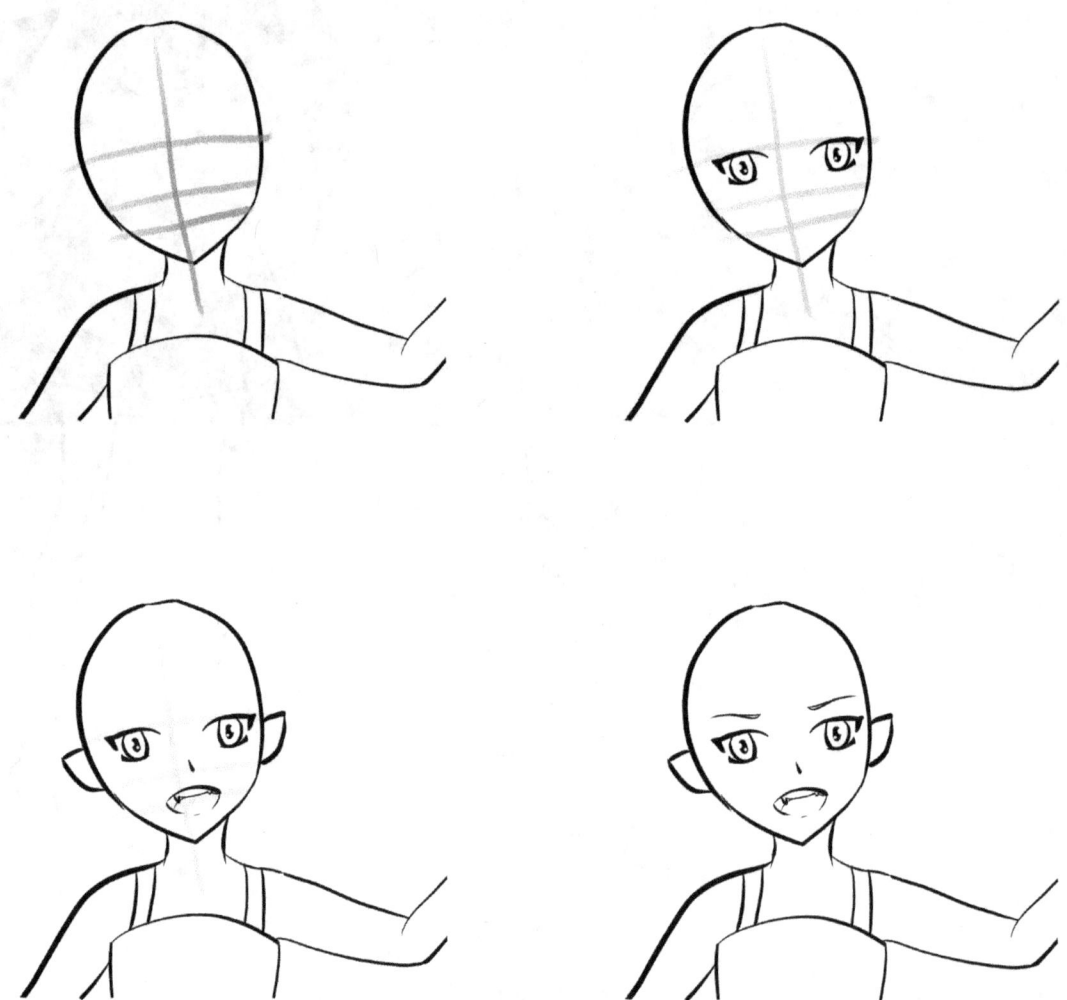

3. Draw the mouth, nose, and ears. If the mouth is open in a smile, you can give her fangs by adding triangles to the line indicating her teeth.

4. Place the eyebrows so that they slant down a little towards the center.

5. Draw in the finer details of the face.

6. Add the hair. The hairstyle can either be something insanely cute and innocent for contrast or something a bit more edgy that can help her look a bit more aggressive.

7. As an extra option, you can add some vampire-themed jewelry.

8. Ink your linework.

9. Add color and shading.

> Your character design can be even more effective if you choose colors that match the theme of vampires.

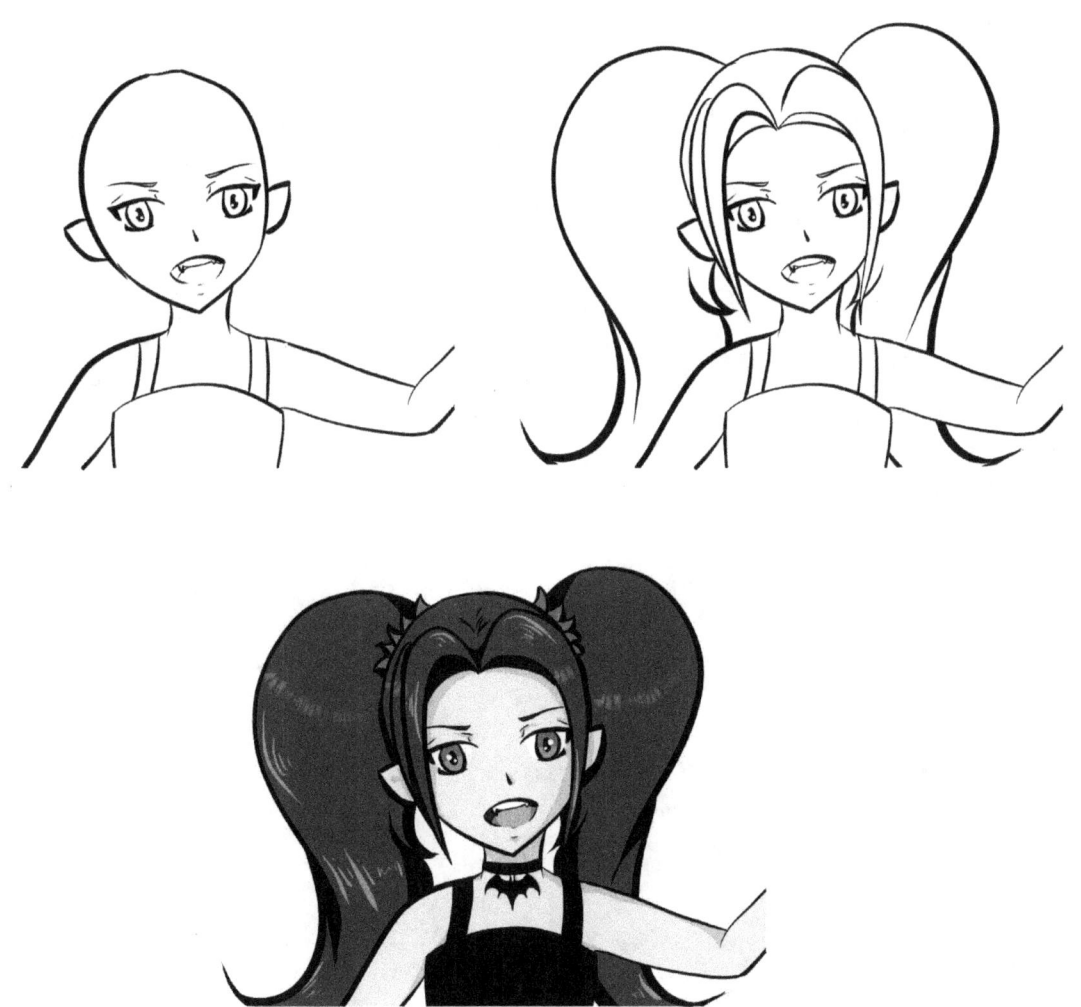

CHAPTER 6

Vengeful Bad Guys

What is an anime without a good villain? It doesn't matter if it's one of those iconic villains you can't help but love, someone who absolutely terrifies, a character you hate with every fiber of your being, one of those villains that you just wish would leave already, a common bully, or someone who's there just to make the plot flow; a good story needs an antagonist! Some anime are even known better for their bad guys than their heroes. Drawing villains can be extremely fun, and you get to do something a little outside the norm.

From the Side

Villains are usually interesting and unique characters who tend to be a bit unconventional. One way to portray this is by showing them from 'out-there' angles, and villains pop up in your manga panels from a side angle quite a lot. This is why it's important to truly master the side profile and some of its finer aspects.

From Boy to Man

You know how to draw a face and how to turn it to a side view, but we've mostly focused on teenagers. This time, we're taking a look at the difference between drawing the head of a teenager and that of an adult. As an example, let's take our teenager from Chapter 4 and see how he grew up.

- The first big difference is the shape. The head is longer and a little narrower. When starting the face, the eye-line is just above the center of the circle. Draw a faint line just a little higher to indicate where the brow will be. Measure the distance between the brow and the top of the circle. Measure the same distance beneath the brow to place your nose-line. Measure the same distance below the nose-line to place the chin-line. The mouth-line is in the middle between the chin and nose-line.

- An adult face is less rounded, the jaw is more prominent, and the chin is wider. This is especially important when viewing from the front. The sides of the face go almost straight

If you want to create a character who's approaching his middle years rather than a young man, you can add light hints of crow's feet, bags under the eyes, and faint wrinkles.

down, and the curve of the jaw is very strong. When drawing the chin, place a short, horizontal line on the chin-line rather than a point to create the chin.

- The mouth is a little wider, and the lower lid is drawn a lot higher to make the eyes look smaller and more mature. The nose is also drawn with stronger lines and sharper edges to make it more prominent.

- The neck is also wider than that of a teenager.

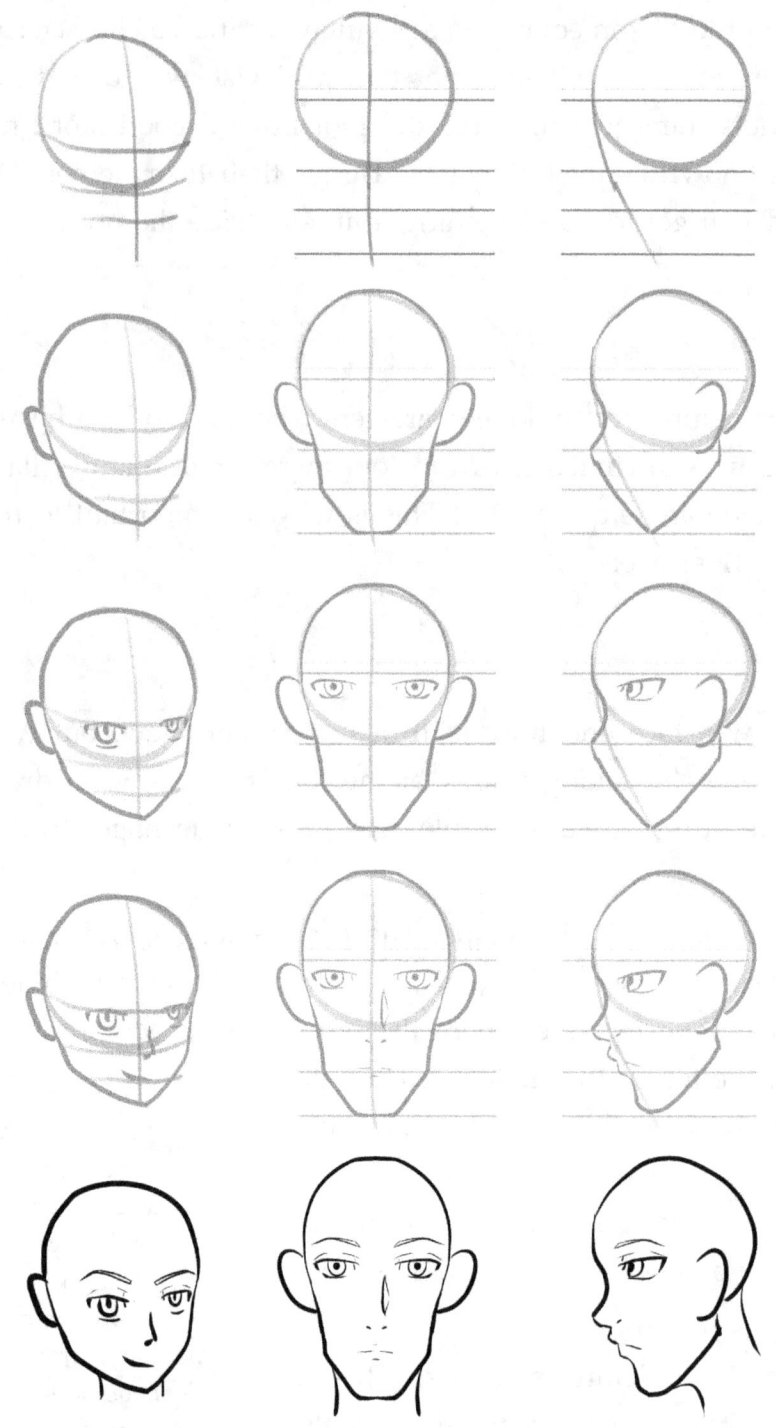

Facial Expressions

While the theory behind drawing facial expressions from the side is the same as from the front, the practical application isn't. The biggest problem is that when viewed from the side, the whole outline of the face changes with the different expressions, such as the brow lowering in a frown or the mouth opening to laugh or shout. Figuring out how to alter the outline like this takes some concentration and won't come naturally from the start. However, mastering these expressions is vital because the right facial expression can turn even the kindest, sweetest looking character into a malicious bad guy hiding in plain sight. To help you get started, though, we'll take a look at some of the more common expressions your villain will be likely to have on their face.

1. Anger

2. Rage

3. Disgust

4. Frustration

5. Evil smile/Plotting smile

6. Evil smirk

7. Evil laugh

Pay close attention to the position of the chin and jaw. If the lips change, so do they.

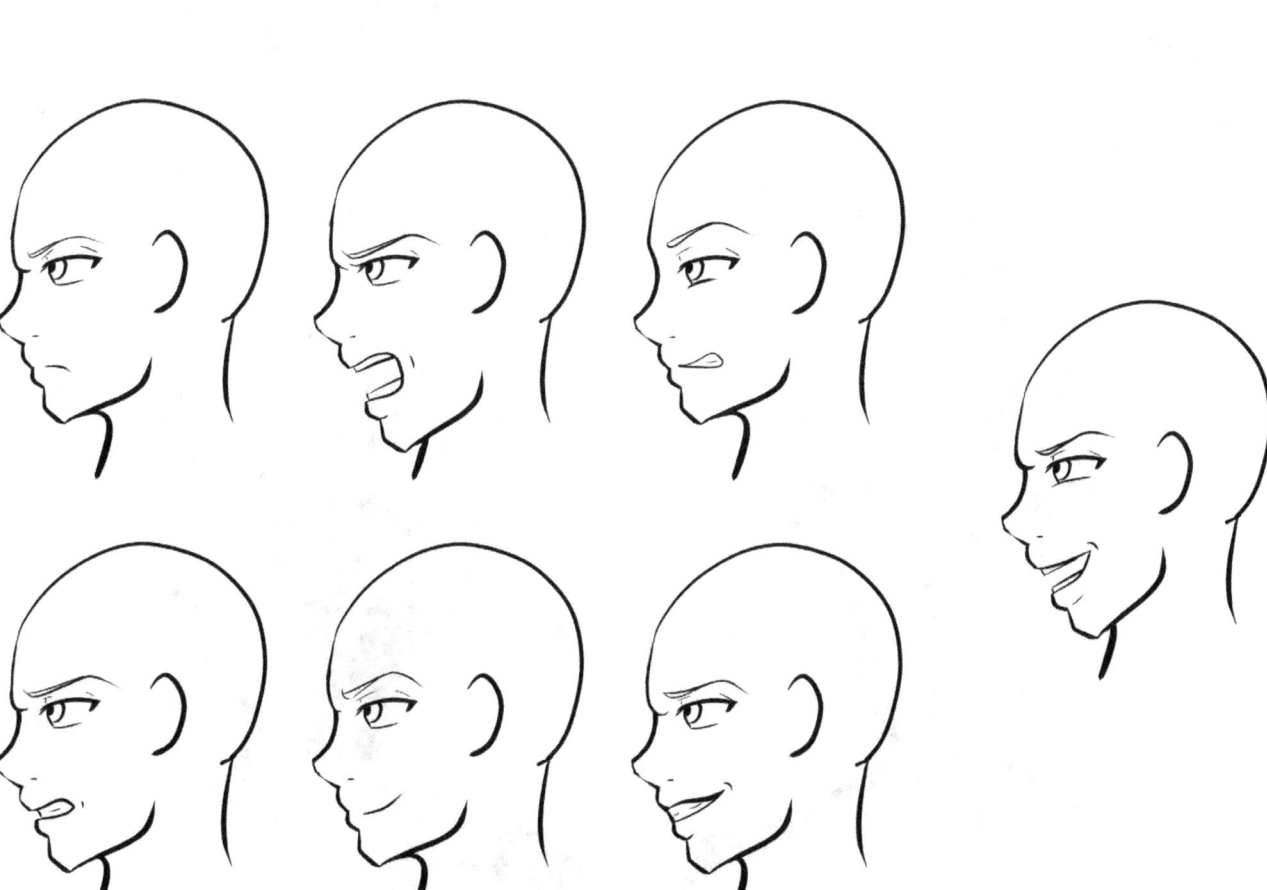

Shading

Shading is your friend when it comes to creating bad guys. Since these villains have a darker personality, you can use more darkness in their appearance to help portray this. Playing with the direction of the light for more ominous shadows and using a little extra shading in the right place can help make your bad guy look even more dangerous and evil. Here are a few examples of the difference a change of shading can do to a character.

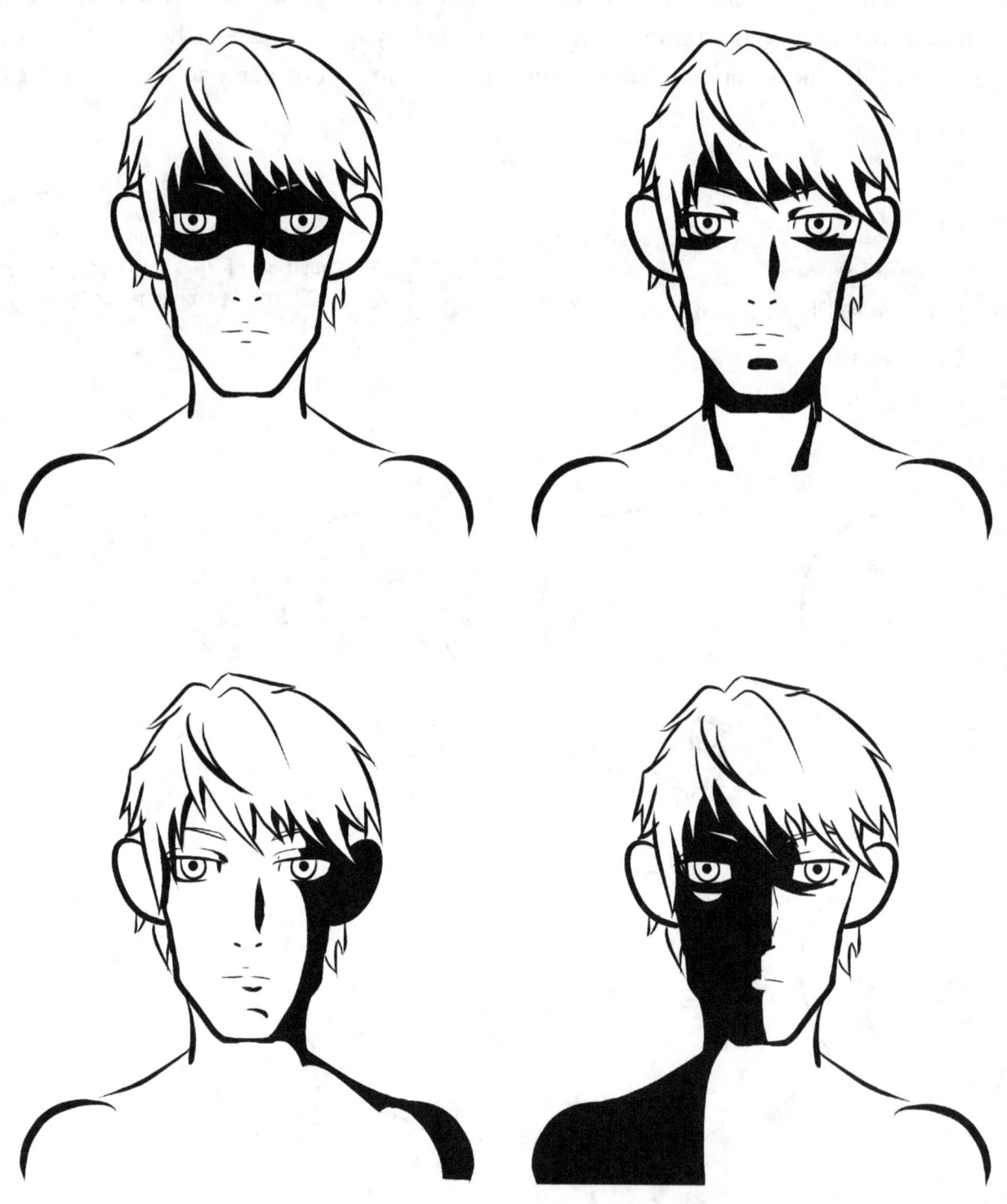

Villainous Features

Every anime and manga have their own way of distinguishing their villains from the rest of the cast. There is no single way to draw a bad guy or make a character look more villainous, but here are a few techniques that many artists like to use for these characters.

1. **Sharper Lines:** By using sharper, harder lines and strengthening corners, it creates a very aggressive, violent mood.

2. **Adding Details:** Adding more details to the face, like outlining the lips or adding cheekbones, often has the strange effect of making a character look more evil.

3. **The Right Expression:** Once again, the right facial expression can convey just how evil a normal-looking character *really* is.

4. **Pose:** The right pose and body language make for a great way to communicate your character's intentions and personality.

5. **Hair:** Some hairstyles are simply better suited for bad guys than others.

6. **Scars:** Giving your character a scar is an excellent way to portray their violent personality and lifestyle.

7. **Clothing:** The right clothing or adjustments to regular clothes can make a huge difference in how your character is portrayed.

In many of your more fantasy and sci-fi-type anime, the bad guys often have strange or interesting markings on their faces.

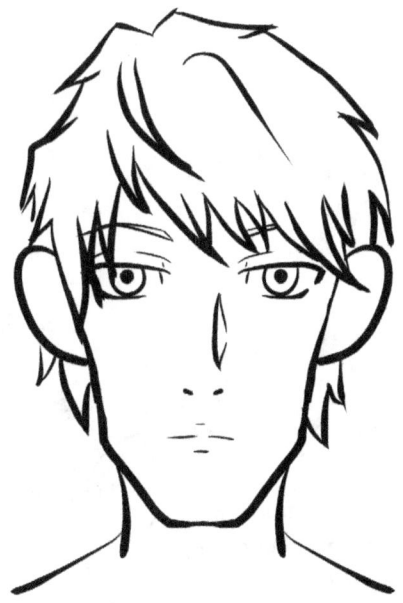

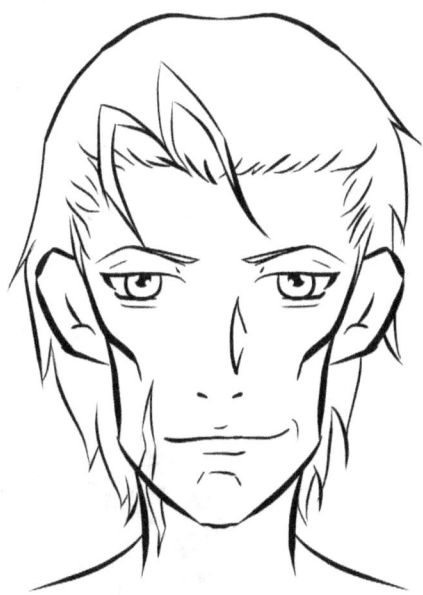

Drawing the Body

Once more, it's time to look at the differences between drawing teenagers and adults.

- Adults are taller, and the head fits into the body seven to eight times.

- The shoulders, chest, and hips are wider.

- The outline of the body has stronger curves.

- The body has more muscle definition.

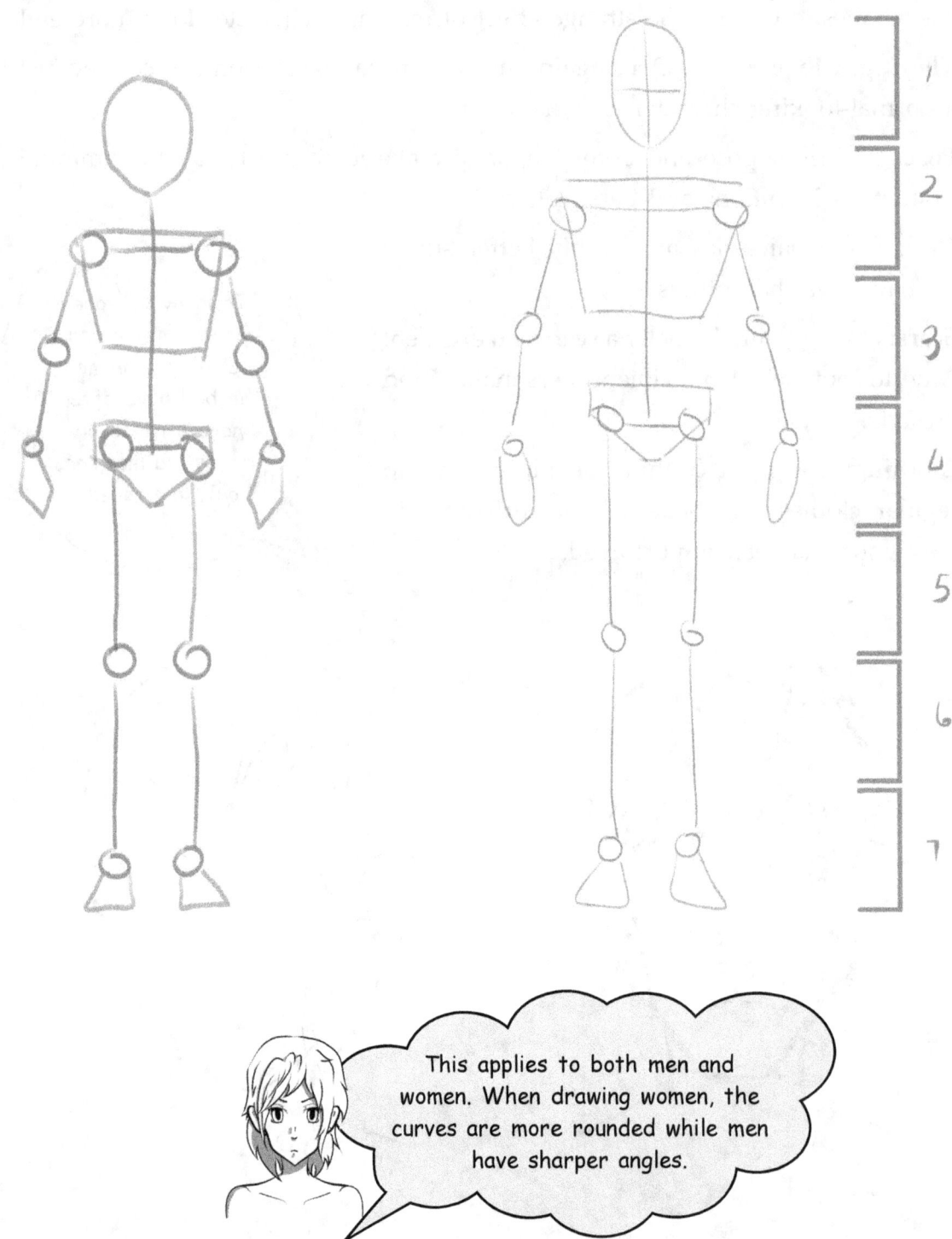

This applies to both men and women. When drawing women, the curves are more rounded while men have sharper angles.

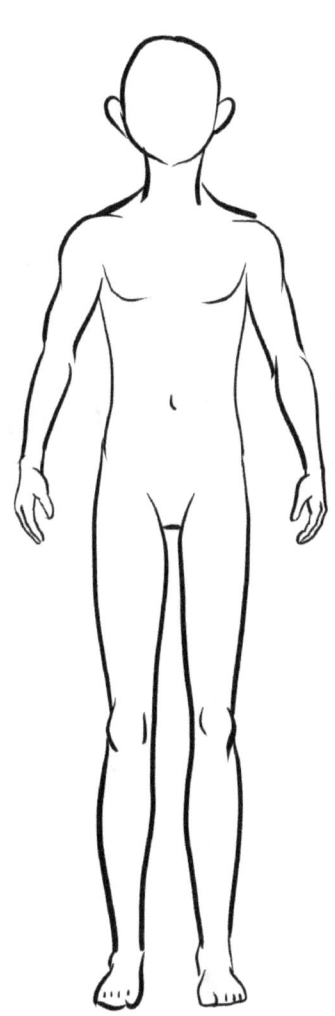
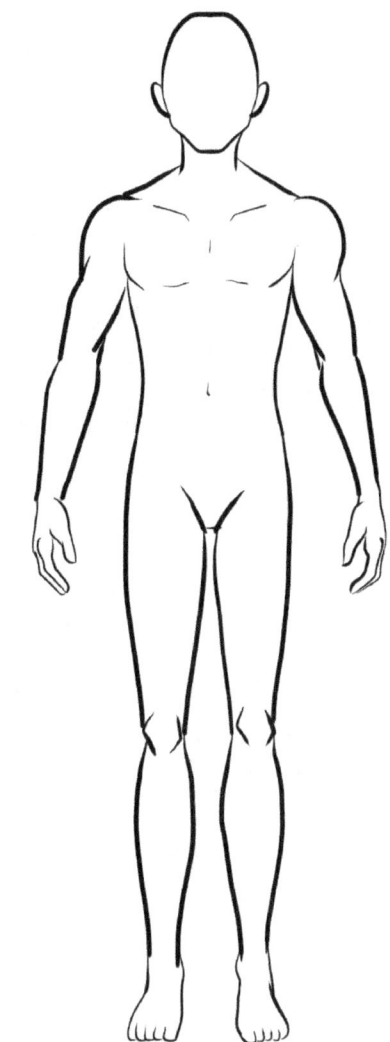

Putting It All Together

Finally, we can get to design the ultimate enemy your protagonist has to face.

1. Map out the basic pose of the body.

2. Put in the torso and hips.

3. Draw the outline of your body.

4. Draw the face and hands.

5. Add the clothing and hair.

6. Put in the final details, and clean up the drawing.

7. Ink your linework

8. Add color and some dramatic shading.

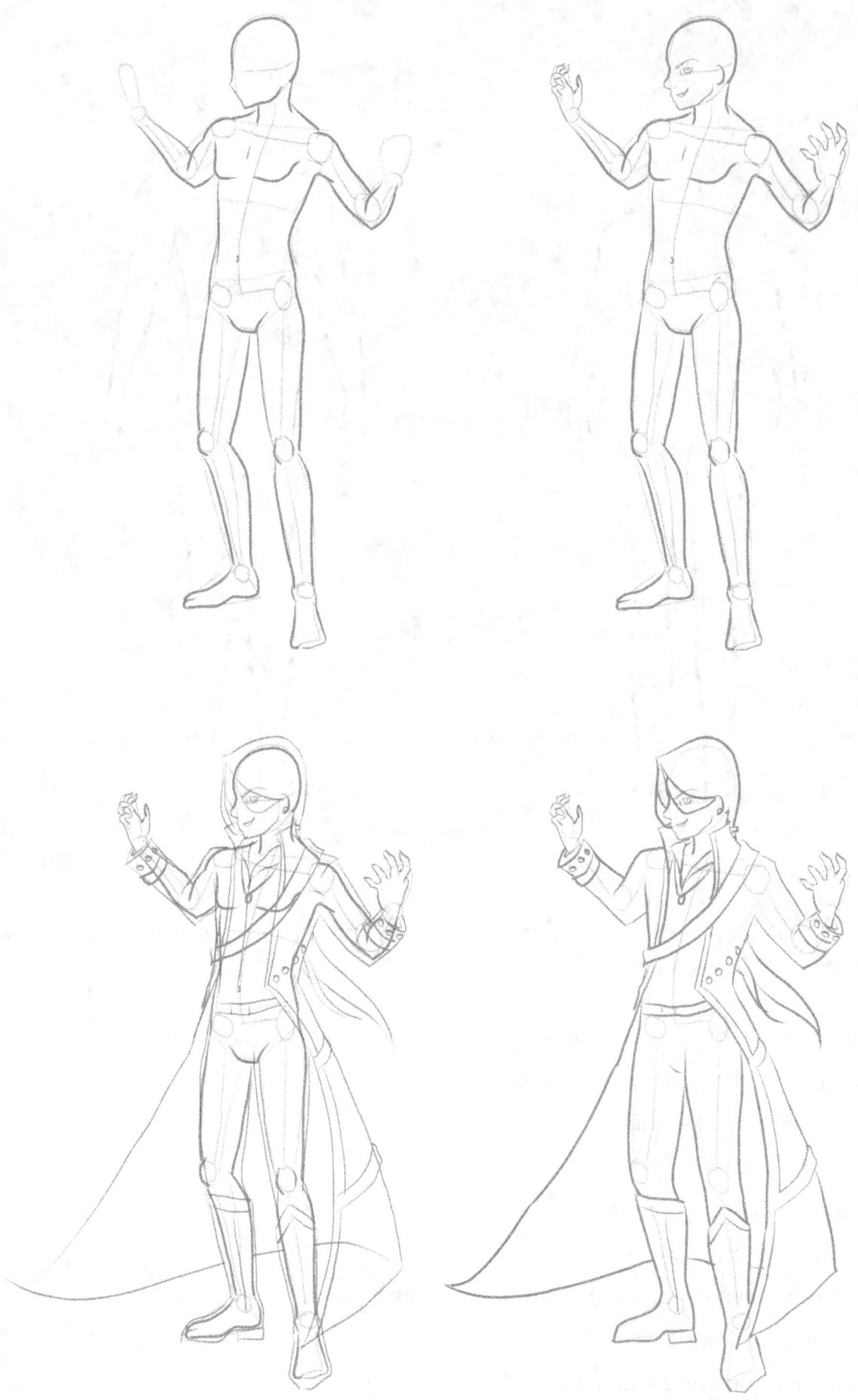

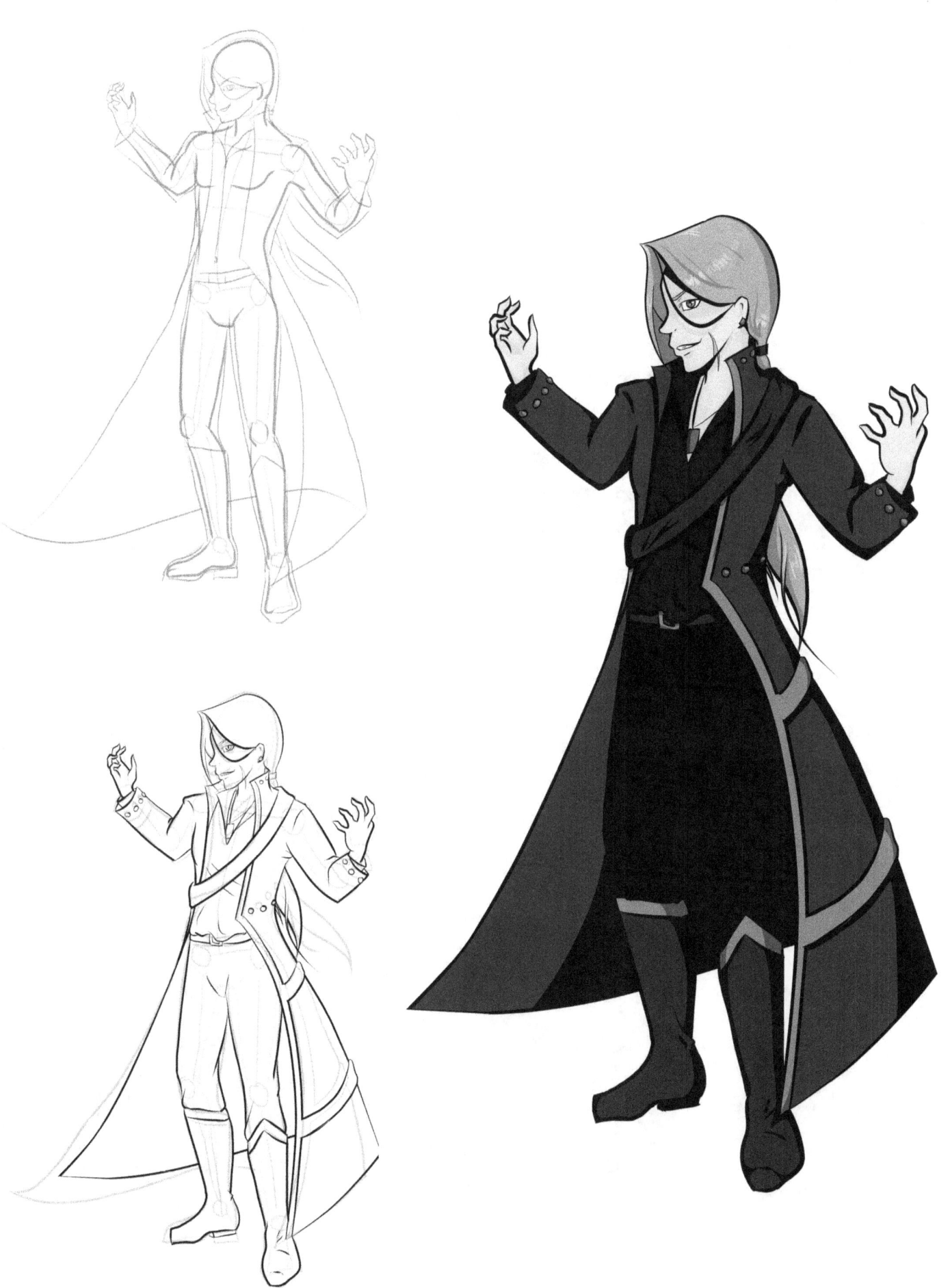

CHAPTER 7

Humorous Personalities

The fan-favorite often makes people laugh the most, be it the main character or a side character. Everyone loves the funny one, and sometimes, characters are created with the specific purpose of being the comic relief.

Always Something to Say

The funny character is always identified the moment they open their mouth. Communication is an important element of creating manga and anime, especially for the character who loves his jokes. Between all the action, the characters, and the background, it can be hard to fit in a space to add the dialogue. This is where the speech bubble comes into play. "Speech bubbles" make it easy to display the dialogue neatly and cleanly and to indicate who is talking. Since there are different types of speech bubbles, you can even indicate which *type* of communication is happening. Here are some of the different types of speech bubbles you'll need to create communication in your manga.

1. **Regular Bubble:** This is the bubble used to indicate regular dialogue. The bubble can either be horizontal or vertical, depending on the space the image allows. The edges of the panel can even cut off some sides.

2. **Thought Bubble:** This bubble is used for the character's thoughts that they aren't speaking out loud. The bubble *doesn't* have a 'tail', and it is usually drawn partially behind the character to whom the thoughts belong.

3. **Double Bubble:** This bubble looks like two regular speech bubbles have been fused together. It is used when everything your character has to say doesn't fit into a single bubble.

4. **Connected Bubbles:** These are bubbles used when a lot of dialogue between two characters is happening in *one* panel. All the speech bubbles of a character are connected to each other.

5. **Off-Panel Bubble:** This bubble with an *inverted* 'tail' indicates that the character speaking *isn't* in the same panel as the speech bubble. Sometimes, if there are a few of these in a single panel, the artist will draw a quick, small sketch of the character's face in the bottom of their speech bubble.

6. **Whispering Bubble:** The bubble has the exact same shape as a speech bubble, but the lines are broken, and it is used to show that a character is talking softly.

7. **Wobbling Bubble:** This bubble is used when a character is very weak or their words are fading away. Wobbly, unsteady lines indicate it.

8. **Inverted Bubble:** This inverted bubble with a black fill and white text is used to portray negative thoughts and emotions. It can also sometimes be used when a character is suddenly saying something very dark or sinister.

9. **Yelling Bubble:** This bubble is drawn using jagged shapes and uneven lines, and it is used to say that the character is yelling in surprise, anger, or fear.

10. **Happy Bubble:** This cloud-shaped bubble is used when a character is being very positive, happy, or hopeful. The 'tail' of the bubble will change into a series of smaller clouds if the character is daydreaming or thinking very happy thoughts.

11. **Announcement Bubble:** This spiky bubble is used to deliver dialogue and official announcements transmitted through television, radio, phones, speakers, and other communication devices.

12. **Narrator Box:** This speech bubble is just a simple box and is used to narrate the story or convey important information to the reader.

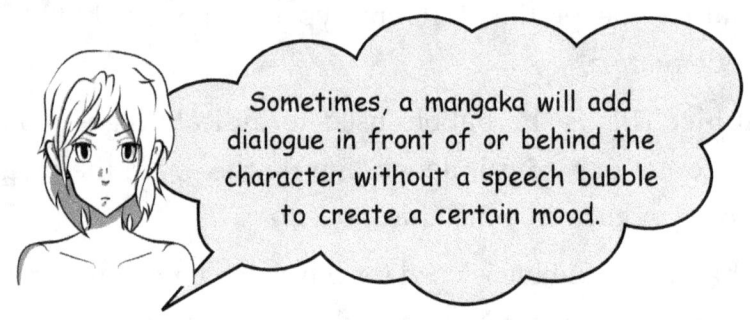

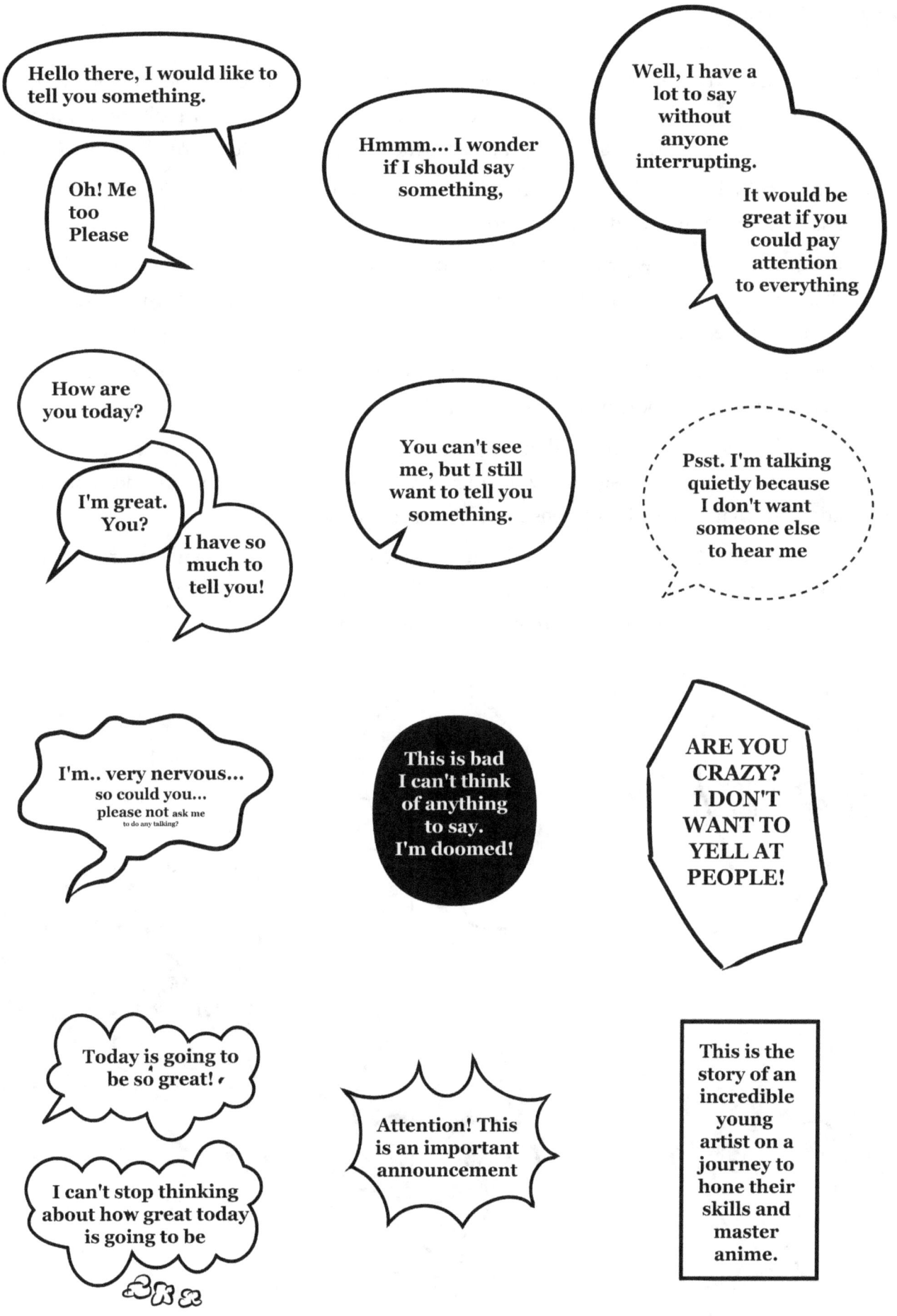

Funny Visuals

The key elements of funny characters are usually their words, actions, and personalities. Still, there *are* a few ways to alter the appearance of a character to make them look more humorous. Once again, there's no 'right' way to do this, and these are simply techniques used to create:

1. **Simplicity:** Funny characters are often drawn very simply, as they are meant to be enjoyed and don't need to be complicated.

2. **Exaggerated Features:** By exaggerating one or two of a character's features, like giving them a big nose, very wide mouth, or ridiculous eyebrows, you can give them a more comical appearance.

3. **Unusual Clothing:** You can make a character look less serious by giving them clothing that seems a little odd or doesn't exactly match their personality.

4. **Rounded Edges:** Just like villains are drawn with sharper edges and harder lines to make them more intense, funny characters are often drawn with soft lines and rounded edges to make them less intense and more relatable.

5. **Irony:** Characters become more humorous when you add visual features that are in contrast with their personality and role, like having a very dangerous, serious female character wear something extremely cute and girly.

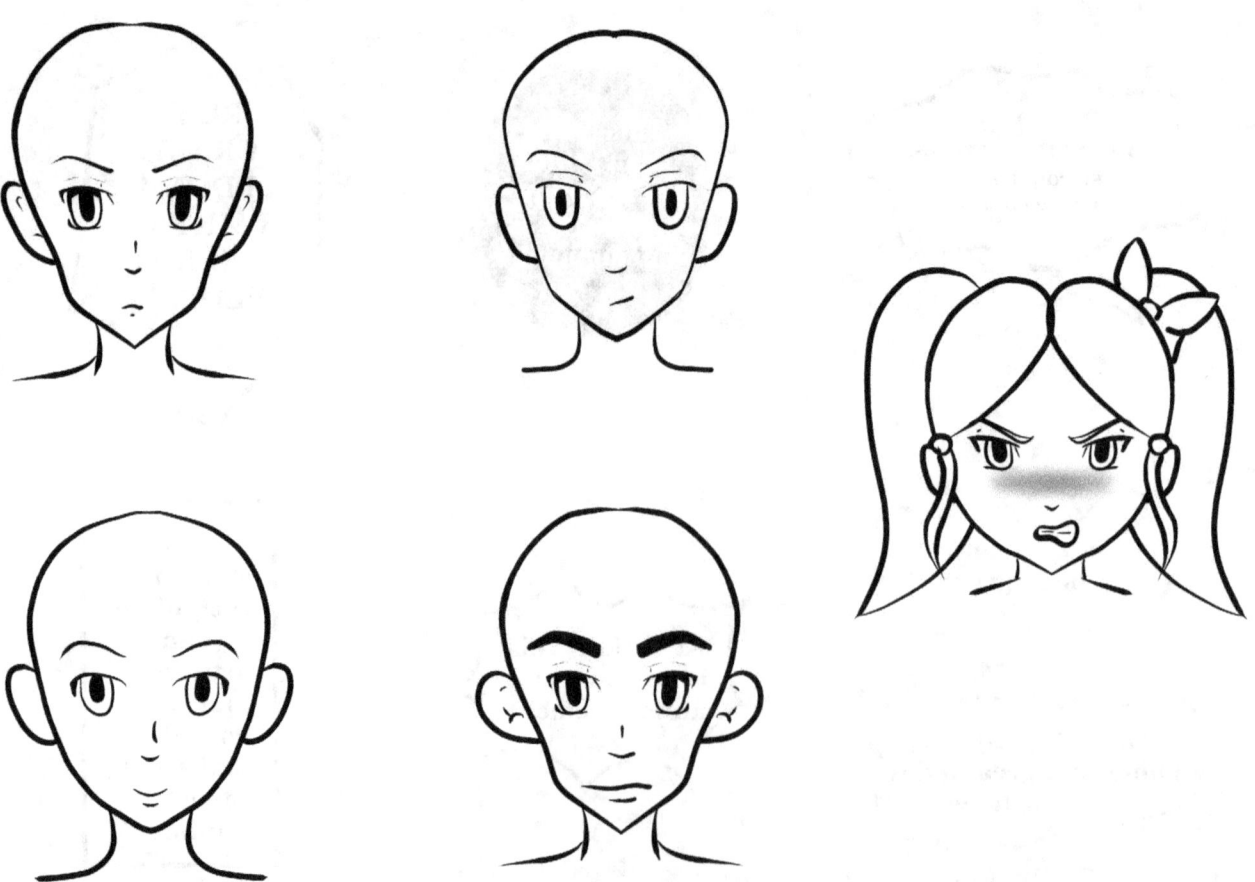

Facial Expressions

Characters with a good sense of humor sometimes have interesting facial expressions and are often seen laughing, so we'll look at some examples of a few funny expressions for your character.

1. **Bursting With Laughter:** The character's eyes are either shut tight or have the lower lid slightly pushed up by the smile. Sometimes, the pupils are very small or completely gone. The mouth is open very wide. You can add tears in the corners or the eyes for an extra touch.

2. **Holding in Laughter:** The eyes are a bit wider than normal, and the pupils are a little smaller. There are sometimes tears in the corner of the eye. The mouth is in a small, tight smile, and the cheeks are bulging out.

3. **Nervous Laughter:** The character is squinting a little or their eyes are closed. They often *don't* make eye contact. The mouth is in an oddly-shaped, wobbly smile. There are usually a few beads of sweat on the forehead and cheeks. If a character is extremely nervous, you can add blue shading to the face from the hairline to just below the eyes.

4. **Dumbfounded:** There are a few ways to do this. For a more 'realistic' expression, the eyes are a little wider and the pupils a little smaller. For a more exaggerated, funny expression, the eyes are either open wide with no iris or pupil, with very small irises, or the pupil is extremely large with no iris. The eyes can also be drawn as plain white circles or small dots. The mouth is usually in a small, straight line.

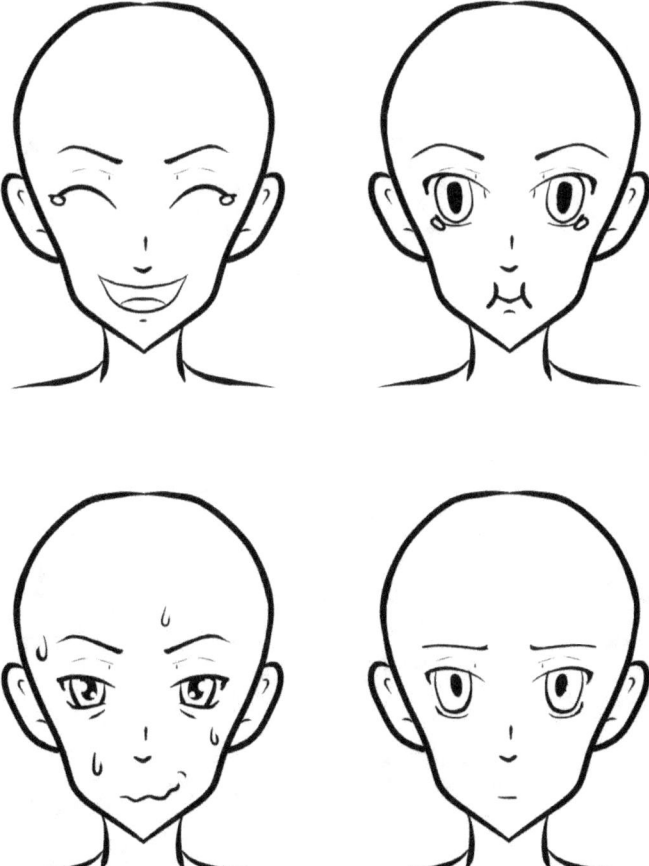

Putting It All Together

Now it's time to put together the comic relief character for our anime.

1. Map out the pose and place the joints.
2. Put in the chest and torso.
3. Flesh out the character, and draw the outline of the body.
4. Draw in the face and hands.
5. Time to add the clothing and hair.
6. Add the final details. Remember to clean up the drawing a little.
7. Ink your linework.
8. Finish with some color and shading.

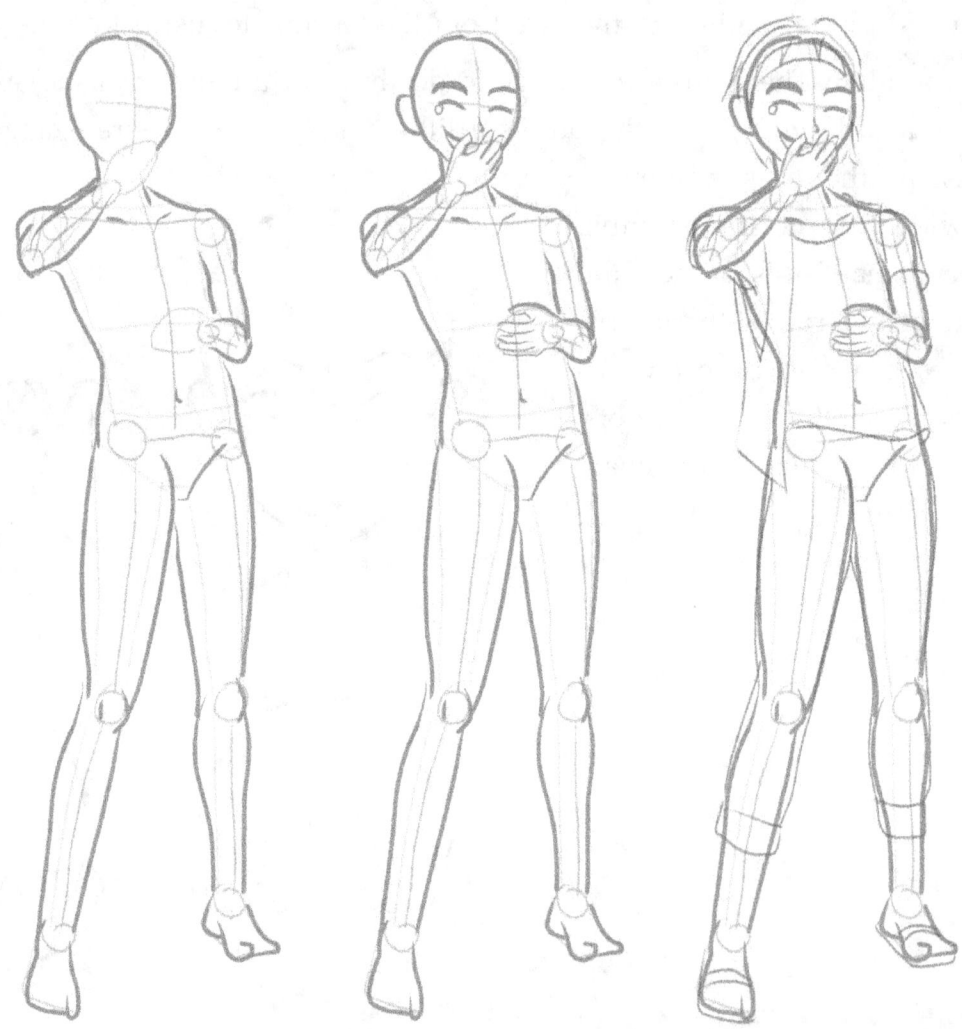

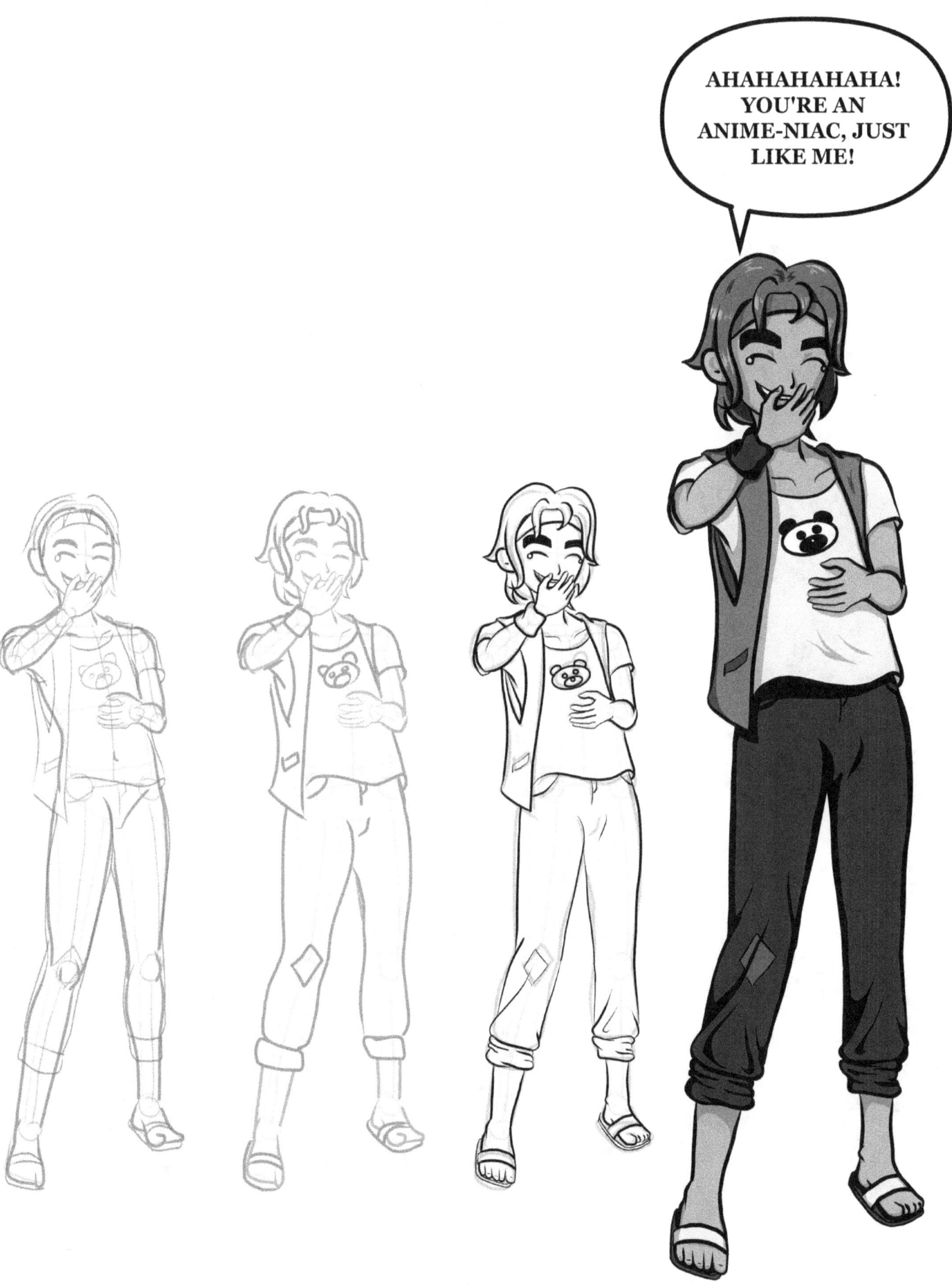

Fantasy Figures

Fantasy is a great genre as it gives you a lot of room to play and lets your imagination run wild. Not only will you be able to play around with the abilities and story of your character, but you can also be creative with their appearance, clothing, and even the *scenery*.

New Shapes

One of the best parts about drawing fantasy is that since you're not limited to *just* humans anymore, you're not limited to human *anatomy*. This is where you can push all the basic proportions and construction to the side and bend—or even break—the rules a little. One of the best ways to do this is to play around with new shapes when drawing faces. Where you'd normally start with a circle and an added chin for a human, you can use an oval or

> When trying new shapes for faces, it's easiest to place the eyes into the shape first and place the rest of the features around them.

just a circle without a chin. You can even abandon round shapes completely and look into squares, rectangles, and triangles. Let your creativity flow and experiment by testing out new shapes.

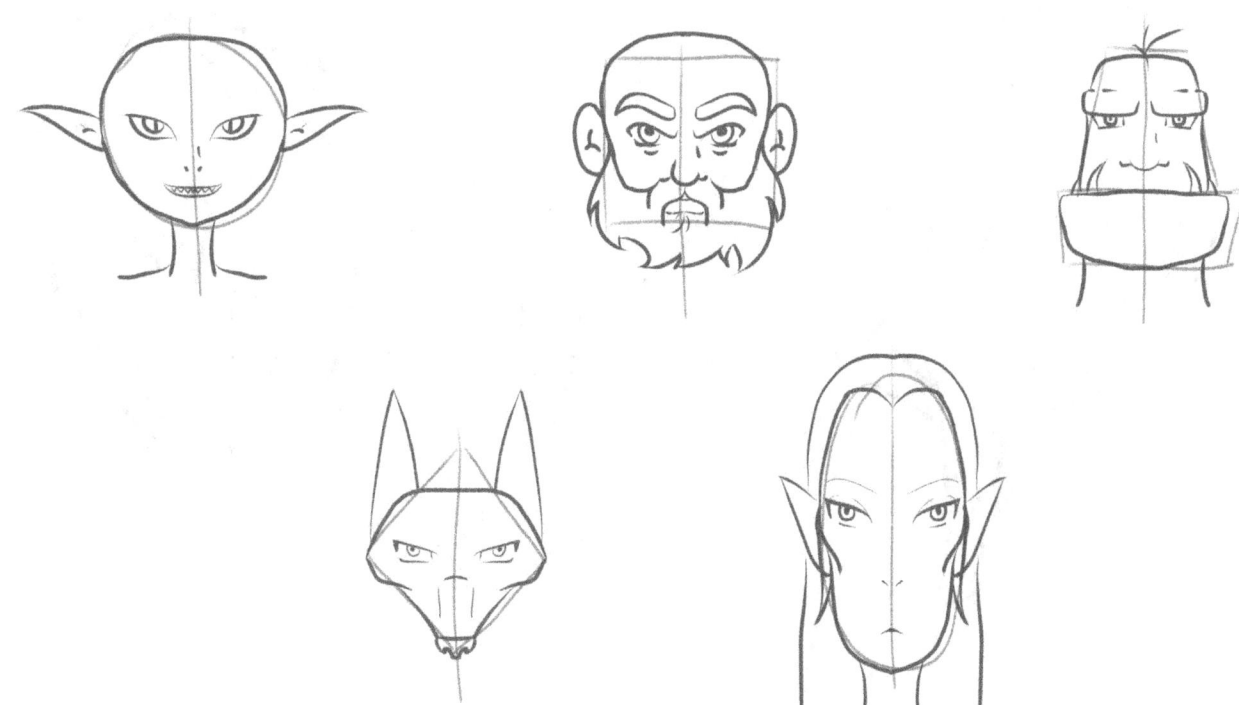

A New World

Your fantasy characters can be whatever you want them to be, and you don't need to stick to mostly human-shaped characters. You can combine human and animal qualities to create interesting creatures like mermaids, harpies, werewolves, or something completely new. You can play around with new shapes and features for hands and feet, like claws, paws, or membranes between the fingers. You can even abandon the human shape entirely and go into more animal-based shapes that have no human features at all.

Furthermore, you can experiment with your clothing and dress your characters in ways you wouldn't normally see, like armor or magical robes. You don't need to limit yourself to a specific culture, style, or even time period. Throw out the normal, and embrace the fantastical!

One thing to remember when drawing fantasy characters is to connect them to reality in small ways. People can more easily relate to characters who have a few human traits with which they can see in themselves and are familiar. If your characters are *too* strange or outlandish, those who see your work won't be able to connect emotionally. This is especially important if you're creating anime or manga where the readers need to get into the story or if you are still new to the art world and people aren't a little more familiar with your work yet.

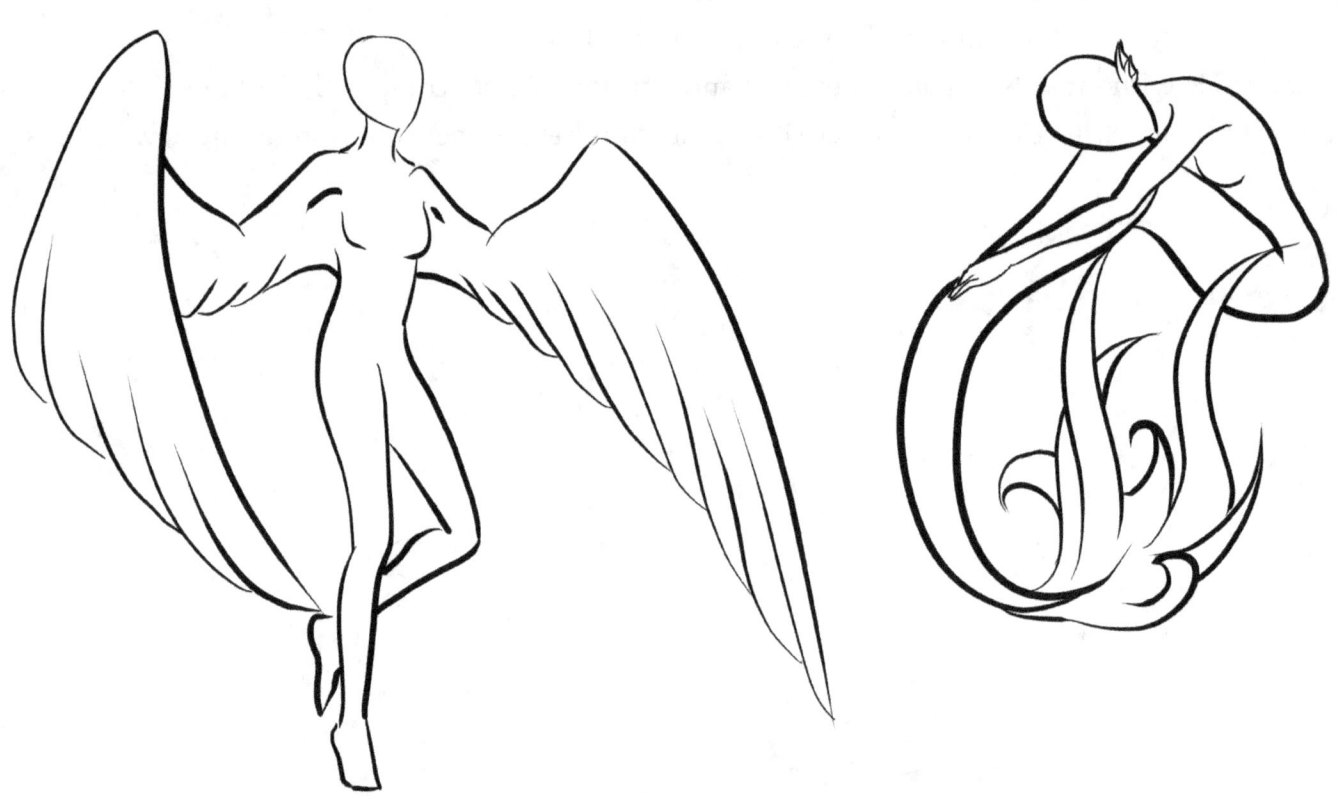

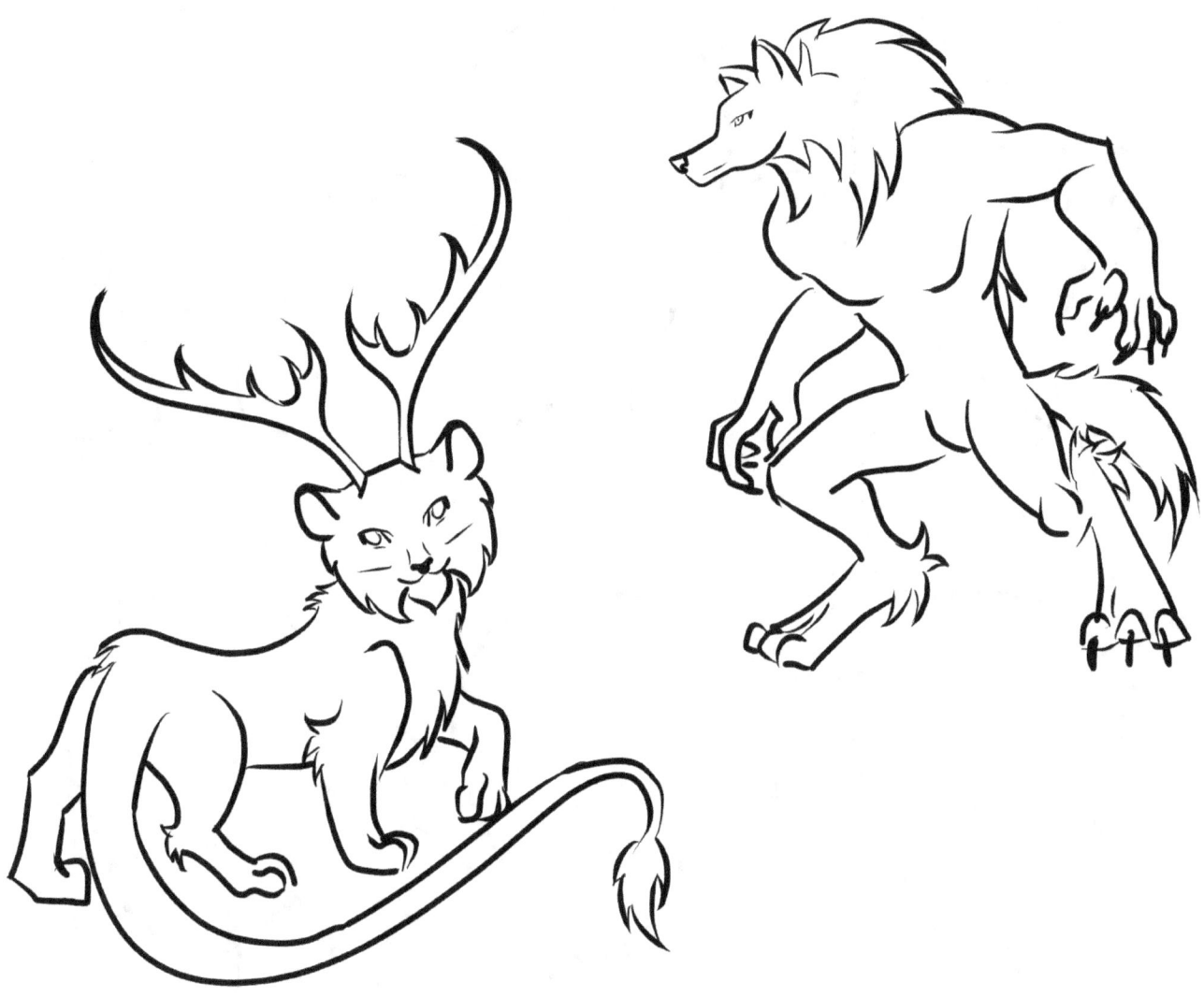

A Head Full of Fantasy

Beyond just the shape, fantasy also lets you add strange, interesting features onto the head.

Horns and Ears

It's always fun to add horns, spikes, antennae, or other similar types of features to your characters. There are lots of different types of horns and antennae, and there's a lot of room to play with their placement and angles. The same goes for ears. You can either alter the normal ear, such as making them a little pointy or giving them long tips, you can replace the ears with something else, like fins or feathers, or you can remove them completely and put a whole new type of ear somewhere else—like the cat girl we created in Chapter 3!

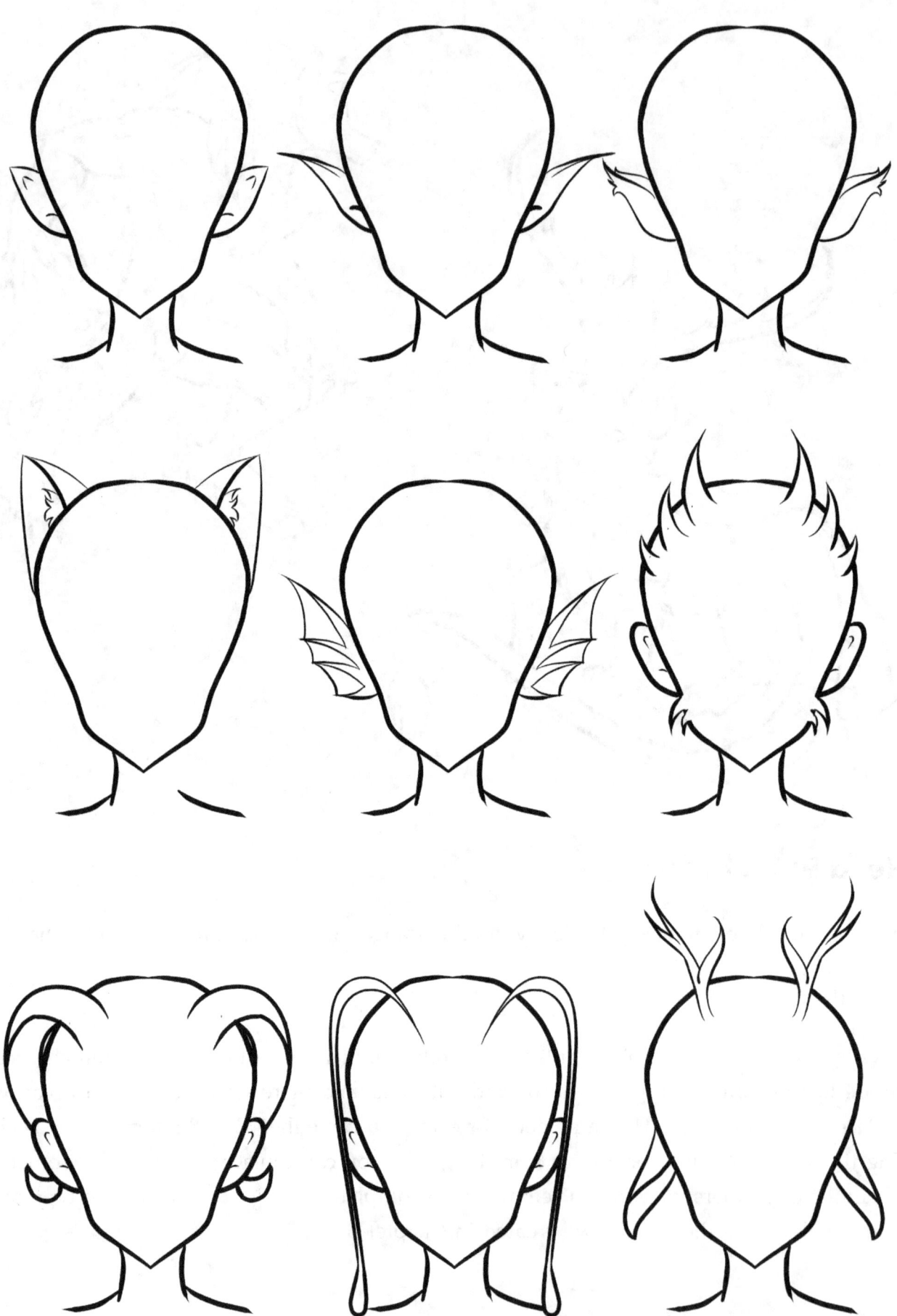

Headgear

Fantasy characters often wear interesting headgear, like wizards' hats, circlets, and helmets. While these may seem very different, they still follow the same process to draw:

1. Draw the basic shape.

2. Refine the outline of all the areas that cover the head, hair, and face.

3. Refine the outline of areas that go behind the head and hair.

4. Add basic details.

5. Refine the drawing, and add the final details.

> With more complex pieces, it's better to work in layers. Start with a base for the headpiece and build onto it layer by layer.

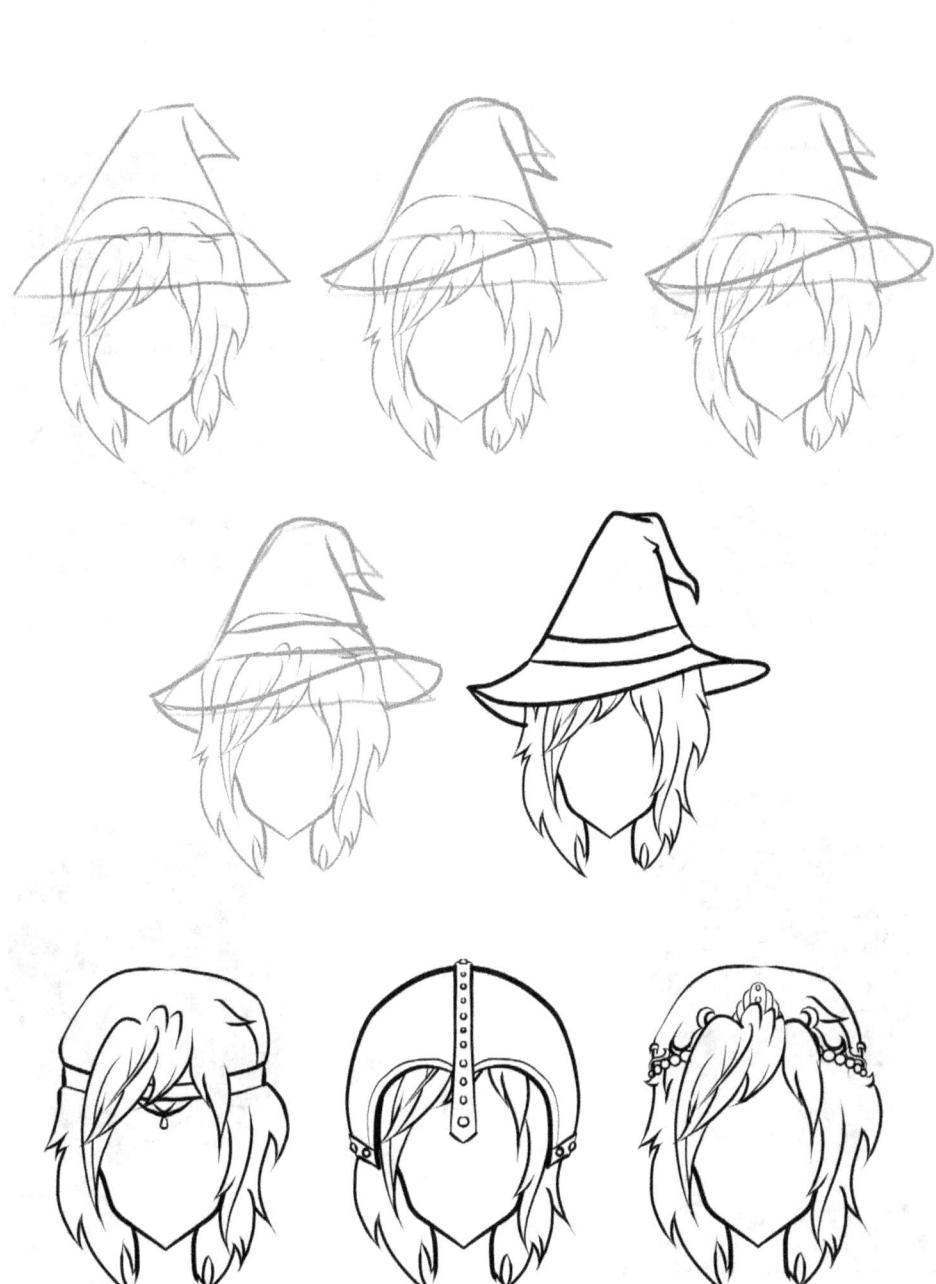

Color

As with everything else in this genre, fantasy gives you even more room to experiment with color. You can be far more bold and creative with your color choices and combinations. Not only are unusual hair and eye colors even *less* out of place than in regular anime, but you can also experiment with more diverse and interesting skin colors. You can even use color to help tell a bit more about the environment they come from, traits specific to their race, and even give hints about their powers and abilities. Clever use of color is also an excellent way of creating magical effects, such as glowing eyes or traces of magical power.

Many fantasy characters often have interesting tattoos and markings on their faces or bodies. This can be a great way to bring in extra color.

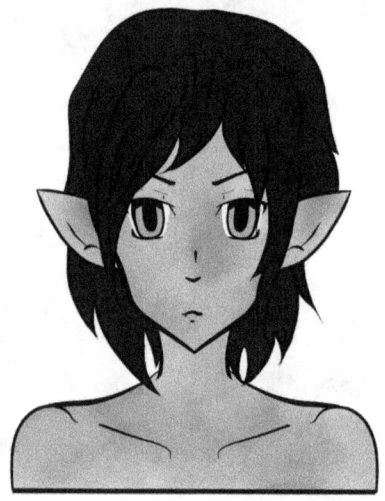

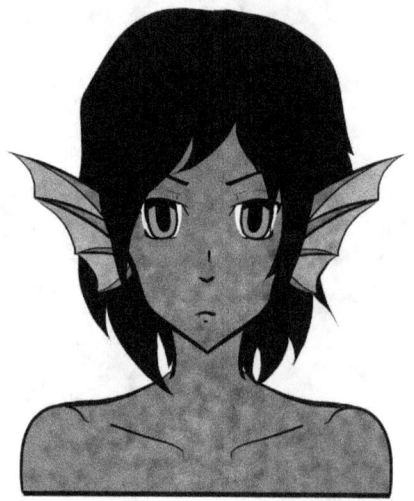

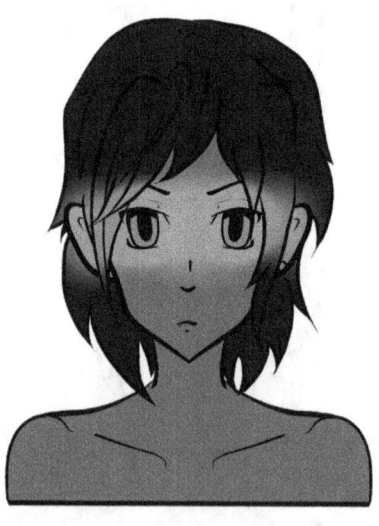

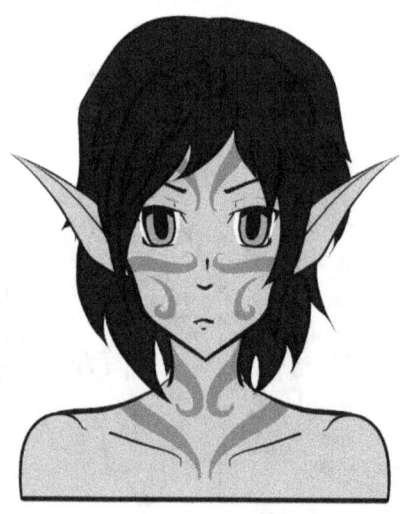

Putting It All Together

It's time to take what we've learned to create a new magical creature. We'll be drawing an elf as an example for this character.

1. Map out the pose, and place the joints.

2. Draw wedge shapes for the torso and hips.

3. Create the outline for the body.

4. Draw in the face and hands.

5. Add the hair and clothingand any interesting extra features if you want.

6. Add all the final details.

7. Refine the drawing and clean it up a little.

8. Ink your linework.

9. Add color and shading.

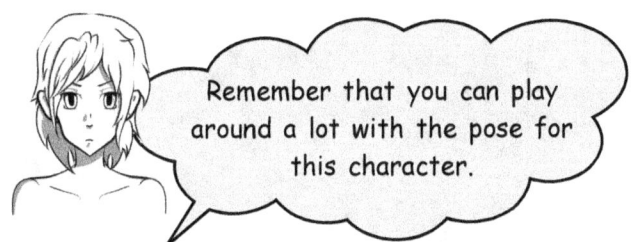

Remember that you can play around a lot with the pose for this character.

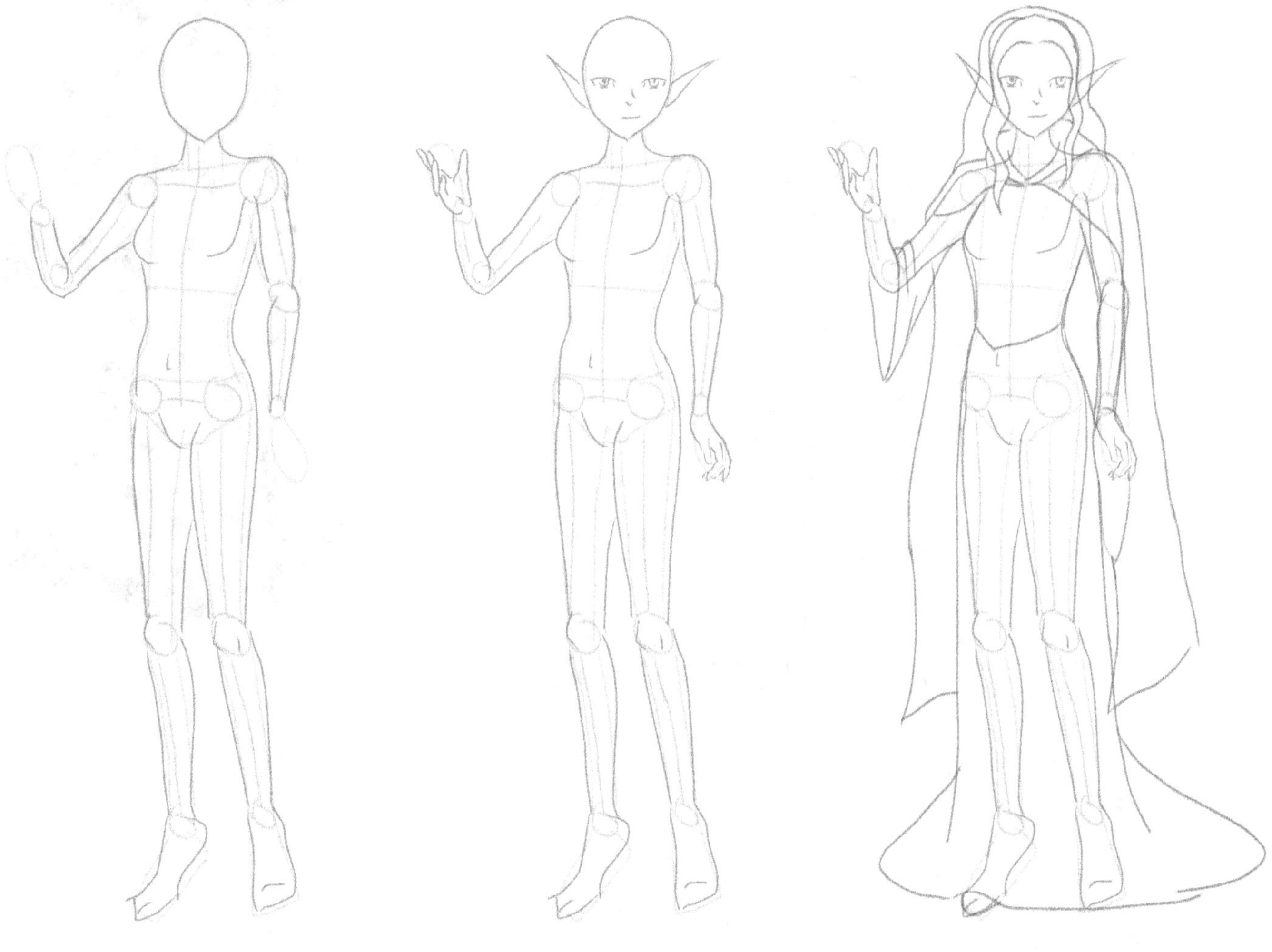

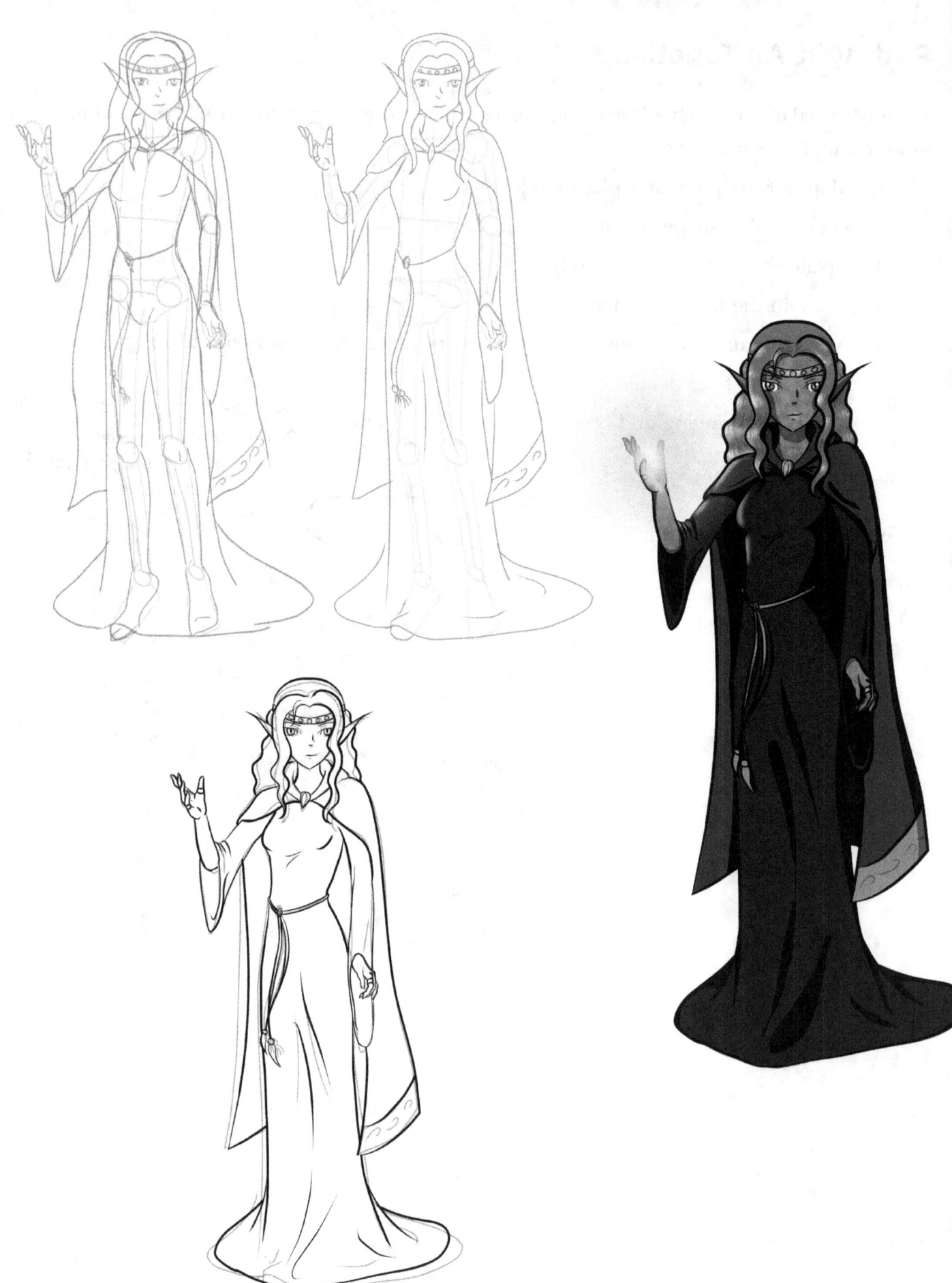

Conclusion

Anime is a great art style that can start off as just the bare minimum and grow into something incredible! You don't need to be an experienced master or an artistic genius to enjoy drawing anime and create amazing characters and artworks. All you need is the basics, and with a bit of practice, patience, and dedication, you can become an amazingly talented artist, and you can even turn your art into a successful career.

We hope you've enjoyed this journey through the world of drawing anime characters and learning a few fundamentals of art. May this be the first step on your path to greatness, and may you find pride and pleasure in the artwork you will be creating from now onwards!

References

5 simple Drawing Exercises for Beginners and Pros. (n.d.). Crave Painting. https://cravepainting. com/blog/simple-drawing-exercisesanimeoutline. (n.d.).

How to Draw an Anime Vampire Girl Step by Step. Anime Outline. https://www.animeoutline. com/how-to-draw-an-anime-vampire-girl-step-by-step/animeoutline. (2012a, October 31).

How to Draw an Anime Girl's Head and Face. AnimeOutline. https://www.animeoutline.com/ how-to-draw-anime-girl-head-and-face/animeoutline. (2012b, November 29).

How to Draw Anime Eyes and Eye Expressions Tutorial. AnimeOutline. https://www.animeoutline. com/how-to-draw-anime-eyes/animeoutline. (2013, April 4).

How to Draw Anime Hands Step by Step. AnimeOutline. https://www.animeoutline.com/how- to-draw-anime-and-manga-hands/animeoutline. (2017a, June 10).

How to Draw Anime Male Body Step By Step Tutorial. AnimeOutline. https://www.animeoutline. com/how-to-draw-an-anime-guy-step-by-step-tutorial/animeoutline. (2017b, June 14).

12 Anime Facial Expressions Chart & Drawing Tutorial. AnimeOutline. https://www.animeoutline. com/12-anime-facial-expressions-chart-drawing-tutorial/animeoutline. (2017c, September 14).

6 Ways to Draw Anime Hands Holding Something. AnimeOutline. https://www.animeoutline. com/draw-anime-hands-holding-something-step-by-step/animeoutline. (2017d, November 20).

How to Draw Anime Clothes. AnimeOutline. https://www.animeoutline.com/how-to-draw- anime-clothing/animeoutline. (2018a, March 1).

How to Draw Male Anime & Manga Eyes. AnimeOutline. https://www.animeoutline.com/how- to-draw-male-anime-eyes/animeoutline. (2018b, April 15).

How to Draw an Anime School Girl in 6 Steps. AnimeOutline. https://www.animeoutline.com/ how-to-draw-anime-school-girl-in-6-steps/animeoutline. (2018c, April 23).

8 Step Anime Boy's Head & Face Drawing Tutorial. AnimeOutline. https://www.animeoutline. com/anime-boy-face-drawing-tutorial/animeoutline. (2018d, May 17).

How to Draw Anime Neck & Shoulders. AnimeOutline. https://www.animeoutline.com/how- to-draw-anime-neck-shoulders/animeoutline. (2018e, June 10).

How to Draw Anime Cat Girl Ears Step by Step. AnimeOutline. https://www.animeoutline.com/how-to-draw-anime-cat-girl-ears-step-by-step/animeoutline. (2018f, June 30).

How to Draw Anime Facial Expressions Side View. AnimeOutline. https://www.animeoutline.com/how-to-draw-anime-facial-expressions-side-view/animeoutline. (2018g, July 17).

How to Draw a Cute Anime Girl Step by Step. AnimeOutline. https://www.animeoutline.com/how-to-draw-cute-anime-girl-step-by-step/animeoutline. (2018h, August 6).

Guide to Picking Colors When Drawing Anime & Manga. AnimeOutline. https://www.animeoutline.com/beginner-guide-to-picking-colors-when-drawing-anime-manga/animeoutline. (2018i, August 14).

10 Step Anime Man's Face Drawing Tutorial. AnimeOutline. https://www.animeoutline.com/anime-man-face-drawing-tutorial/animeoutline. (2018j, September 4). How to Draw an Anime Boy Full Body Step by Step. AnimeOutline. https://www.animeoutline.com/how-to-draw-an-anime-boy-full-body-step-by-step/animeoutline. (2018k, November 3).

How to Shade an Anime Face in Different Lighting. AnimeOutline. https://www.animeoutline.com/how-to-shade-an-anime-face-in-different-lighting/animeoutline. (2018l, November 16).

How to Draw Female Anime Eyes Tutorial. AnimeOutline. https://www.animeoutline.com/how-to-draw-female-anime-eyes/animeoutline. (2018m, December 15).

How to Draw Anime & Manga Arms Tutorial. AnimeOutline. https://www.animeoutline.com/how-to-draw-anime-arms/animeoutline. (2019a, April 16).

How to Draw Manga Speech Bubbles Tutorial. AnimeOutline. https://www.animeoutline.com/how-to-draw-manga-speech-bubbles/animeoutline. (2019b, July 19).

How to Draw Anime Muscular Male Body Step by Step. AnimeOutline. https://www.animeoutline.com/how-to-draw-anime-muscular-male-body-step-by-step/animeoutline. (2019c, October 11).

How to Draw Anime Hats & Head Ware. AnimeOutline. https://www.animeoutline.com/how-to-draw-anime-hats/animeoutline. (2020a, February 20).

How to Draw Anime Poses Step by Step. AnimeOutline. https://www.animeoutline.com/how-to-draw-anime-poses-step-by-step/animeoutline. (2020b, March 13).

How to Shade Anime Hair Step by Step. AnimeOutline. https://www.animeoutline.com/how-to-shade-anime-hair-step-by-step/animeoutline. (2020c, April 23).

How to Draw an Anime Elf Girl Step by Step. AnimeOutline. https://www.animeoutline.com/how-to-draw-anime-elf-girl-step-by-step/animeoutline. (2020d, May 19).

How to Draw Anime Skirts Step by Step. AnimeOutline. https://www.animeoutline.com/how-to-draw-anime-skirts-step-by-step/Canson Studio. (n.d.).

Manga: Selecting your paper | L'atelier Canson. Www.cansonstudio.com. https://www.cansonstudio.com/manga-selecting-your-paperCinder Block Studios. (2015, February 16).

Everything You Need to Know About...Drawing Inks. Www.youtube.com. https://www.youtube.com/watch?app=desktop&v=oLoAebqmnWQConcept Art Empire. (2016, June 21).

Why Is It Important To Practice Fundamentals First? Concept Art Empire. https://conceptartempire.com/why-fundamentals-first/DokiDokiDrawing. (2019, April 16).

Tools of a Manga Artist: BRUSH PEN. Www.youtube.com. https://www.youtube.com/watch?app=desktop&v=ANiWW5tCM4QDrawfee Show. (2017, December 22).

Artists Draw the Ultimate Anime Villain. Www.youtube.com. https://www.youtube.com/watch?app=desktop&v=ELdvoFRHmdkeHow. (2009, May 6).

Drawing & Illustration Lessons : How to Draw Fantasy Figures. Www.youtube.com. https://www.youtube.com/watch?app=desktop&v=0ZbKhAB9zggFlax Art Design. (n.d.).

Ink Buying Guide | Learn about Drawing Inks | FLAX art. Flaxart.com. https://flaxart.com/ink-buying-guide/G, A. (2020, October 30).

7 Best Inking Pens for Comics & Manga [Reviews+Buyer's Guide]. Architecture Lab. https://www.architecturelab.net/best-inking-pens/Gvaat. (n.d.).

How to Draw Anime Expressions, Keys to Conveying Emotion in Drawing – GVAAT'S WORKSHOP. Gvaat.com. https://www.gvaat.com/blog/how-to-draw-anime-expression-the-keys-to-conveying-emotion-in-drawing/Jazza. (2015, May 26).

How to Practice - Improve your Art Skills, the Smart Way! Www.youtube.com. https://www.youtube.com/watch?app=desktop&v=Bu3ulVhO3z4Lee, L. (2018, March 28).

Best 10 Markers for Drawing Manga. ANIME Impulse TM. https://www.animeimpulse.com/blog/2019/3/28/best-10-markers-for-drawing-mangaLewis, C. L. (2015, September 5).

5 Curving Line Drawing Exercises. Carrie L. Lewis, Artist. https://www.carrie-lewis.com/5-curving-line-drawing-exercises/Lewis, C. L. (2021, April 17).

Straight Line Drawing Exercises. Carrie L. Lewis, Artist. https://www.carrie-lewis.com/straight-line-drawing-exercises/LZM Studio. (2016, February 19).

More Details About Soft Lead vs Hard Lead Pencils. Www.youtube.com. https://www.youtube.com/watch?app=desktop&v=jLrnDFN7nZImarkcrilley. (2013a, February 23).

How to Draw a Bad Guy, Manga Style (Narrated Version). Www.youtube.com. https://www.youtube.com/watch?app=desktop&v=2BXmWDZqNCcmarkcrilley. (2013b, February 23).

How to Draw a Bad Guy, Manga Style (Narrated Version). Www.youtube.com. https://www.youtube.com/watch?app=desktop&v=2BXmWDZqNCcmarkcrilley. (2018, December 7).

How to Draw Manga Faces: Child vs. Teen. Www.youtube.com. https://www.youtube.com/watch?app=desktop&v=5fUxYuAzWPwMay, T. (2021, March 12).

The best mechanical pencils for artists and designers. Creative Bloq. https://www.creativebloq.com/buying-guides/the-best-mechanical-pencils-for-artists-and-designersmikeymegamega. (2018a, February 24).

MAPPING THE FACE FOR ANIME & MANGA. Www.youtube.com. https://www.youtube.com/watch?app=desktop&v=_05or04sGAomikeymegamega. (2018b, July 13).

How To Draw CHILDREN FOR ANIME MANGA. Www.youtube.com. https://www.youtube.com/watch?app=desktop&v=bj9qos_BEoEMiriam. (2016, August 23).

The Best Nibs for Drawing Manga | JetPens. Www.jetpens.com. https://www.jetpens.com/blog/the-best-nibs-for-drawing-manga/pt/893MIRO. (2017, January 21).

How To Draw CHILD, TEEN, and ADULT (ANIME) - Step By Step. Www.youtube.com. https://www.youtube.com/watch?v=0C2-YjoLSfUMkiss L VARTIST. (2019, August 31).

How to draw Anime "Hair" NO TIMELAPSE [Anime Drawing Tutorial for Beginners]. Www.youtube.com. https://www.youtube.com/watch?app=desktop&v=bitMwOMjNR4Painter. (n.d.).

Painter 2021 | Download Your Free Trial. Www.painterartist.com. https://www.painterartist.com/en/tips/draw-anime/faces/Pen & Blade. (2018, August 30).

How to Draw Fantasy Faces Course. Www.youtube.com. https://www.youtube.com/watch?app=desktop&v=RfTb17tc5zYShinigami Arts. (2020, May 31).

How To Draw Manga "Basic Anatomy"MAPPING THE FACE. Www.youtube.com. https://www.youtube.com/watch?app=desktop&v=-VYXy_J1hDMStaff, A. N. (2017, July 7).

The Beginning Artist's Guide to Perspective Drawing. Artists Network. https://www.artistsnetwork.com/art-mediums/learn-to-draw-perspective/Vermillion Art. (2016, June 12).

Tutorial Tuesdays: Male/Female drawing differences | Anime Amino. Anime | Aminoapps.com. https://aminoapps.com/c/anime/page/blog/tutorial-tuesdays-male-female-drawing-differences/70tP_u86o4jb1MPVZppdgaVXNR0waLZagrobelna, M. (2018, November 8).

How to Draw Anime Heads and Faces. Design & Illustration Envato Tuts+. https://design.tutsplus.com/tutorials/how-to-draw-anime-heads-and-faces--cms-31884

www.ingramcontent.com/pod-product-compliance
Lightning Source LLC
Chambersburg PA
CBHW081604220526
45468CB00010B/2761